Political Prisoner 3/75

of

DR H KAMUZU BANDA OF MALAWI

by Sam Mpasu

 AFRICAN PUBLISHING GROUP

African Publishing Group
P.O. Box 350
Harare, Zimbabwe

© Sam Mpasu 1995
First Published by APG 1995

Cover Concept:	David Martin
Cover Design:	Inkspot Design Studio
DTP:	Violet Mashaire
Printed by:	Jongwe Press

ISBN 1-77901-089-3

Contents

About The Author

Sam Mpasu is Minister of Education, Science and Technology and Member of Parliament for Ntcheu Central constituency in Malawi and Chief Whip in Parliament.

He insists that he is in politics by accident. He never thought that he would ever end up in politics, certainly not under Dr Hastings Kamuzu Banda's one-party dictatorship. The only way to remove his rule was to replace it, otherwise he was going to come back with more viciousness. That is why Sam Mpasu thought that winning the referendum for multiparty democracy was not enough. The elections had to be contested and won.

Sam Mpasu was a civil servant when, in 1975, five policeman from the Special Branch picked him up from his office in Blantyre. That was the beginning of a two-year imprisonment, without trial or charges, which is the subject matter of this book. While in the notorious Mikuyu Maximum Security Prison, Malawi's equivalent to Robben island, Mpasu promised himself that if ever the opportunity arose for him to contribute, however little, towards the removal of Dr Banda's cruel and inhuman dictatorship, then he would do so with all his heart.

The opportunity arose in 1991 when Bakili Muluzi, a business-man and a former Secretary-General of the Malawi Congress Party, secretly approached him to join an underground movement which Mluzi had just founded. Its name was the United Democratic Party. Its main weapon was midnight leaflets. Dr Banda's Malawi Congress Party was soon shaken to the roots as its legitimacy to rule Malawi was constantly questioned and undermined. Calls by the donor community for respect for human rights and the rule of law hastened the collapse of the dictatorship.

In October 1992, the United Democratic Party came out in the open, but as a pressure group, called the United Democratic Front (UDF). It was called by the name because it was still unconstitutional and therefore treasonable for any political party other than the Malawi Congress Party to exist. In addition, it was considered risky on account of the many seditious things which had been published in the name of the United Democratic Party. Sam Mpasu became the first Editor-In-Chief of UDF News which could now exist legally. It pulled no punches and got banned, only to be reinstated after a court challenge.

On 14 June 1993, a referendum was held to decide whether or not Malawi should revert to a multi-party system after the thirty years of a single-party dictatorship. Sam Mpasu sat on the Referendum Commission. Dr Banda lost. Over two-thirds of the electorate rejected the single-party dictatorship.

The results of the referendum made it possible for the pressure groups to become legitimate political parties. Parliamentary and presidential elections were called for 17 May 1994. They were contested by eight political parties, including the Malawi Congress Party. Out of the eight, only three political parties won seats in parliament. The UDF won both the presidential and parliamentary elections. Sam Mpasu won his parliamentary seat and was appointed to the Cabinet by President Bakili Muluzi.

Sam Mpasu is married to Linda. His first marriage to Sophia was destroyed by his long imprisonment. He has seven children, three from his first marriage, two with Linda and two were adopted from her.

Introduction

The story and characters in this book are true. Although it may read like fiction, it is not. Everything is factual and every incident actually happened. I make no apology to anyone.

For a long time I was urged by friends to write about my nasty experience in Dr Banda's prisons. I resisted the temptation to do so. They gave me a very good reason. They said that my story would help to prick the conscience of many people and would force them to do something to moderate or even eliminate the inhuman cruelties of Dr Hastings Kamuzu Banda's dictatorial rule.

I, too, had a very good reason for resisting the temptation to write the story. I knew better. Most likely, the book would have been banned promptly by the Censorship Board and I would have considered myself very lucky to be thrown into jail again. Now that Dr Banda's Life Presidency of Malawi has been terminated by mightier forces than my pen, the story can be told safely.

I am fortunate and very grateful to the Almighty God that I came out of Dr Banda's jails alive. I am also grateful that I have had the opportunity to participate in the democratization process of Malawi which Dr Banda failed to stop and which ultimately defeated him.

I have written this book with the fond hope that Malawians in particular, and Africans in general, will learn about the dangers of allowing one person to hold too much power.

My deep gratitude goes to my secretary, Mrs Ruth Mitochi, and Miss Christine Mayini for typing the manuscript and making valuable suggestions.

This book is dedicated to all those Malawians who perished in jail, out of jail and in exile, for fighting for basic human rights in Malawi.

CHAPTER 1

The Arrest

All my life I had thought that jails were only for criminals. My understanding was that only the courts could send a person to jail. It is true that I had heard of detention-without-trial but I had never connected detention with imprisonment. My understanding was that a detainee was different from a prisoner; that a detainee could not be put into prison with convicted prisoners. I did not even imagine that a person who had not been charged with any offence could be thrown into prison and treated worse than a convicted prisoner.

Imprisonment-without-trial, in my view, was something which was so manifestly unjust that even primitive tribes did not use it. At least no anthropologist had told me that there was a primitive tribe anywhere in the world which had prisons or used them to lock up innocent people.

I was, admittedly, naive. I had overlooked the fact that our so-called modern and civilised world sometimes does things which primitive tribes would be ashamed of. Dr Hastings Banda, the then Life-President of Malawi, is an educated man by any standards. He has a chain of degrees from Meharry, Chicago and other universities in America and Edinburgh in Scotland. He certainly had schooling. Whether schooling and education are one and the same thing is a different matter. Anyhow, many people around the world had expected him to be able to run a small nation of four million inhabitants in a civilised manner. In the final analysis he was not much better in his brutality than other African leaders who had barely completed primary school. He, more than anyone else, convinced me that schooling and education are different things.

My dreams were shattered on Tuesday, 22 January 1975.

1

On that day I learned the painful lesson that one did not have to break any law in order to be sent to jail. That was not the only lesson I learned. The second lesson was that in a dictatorship legal formalities were not necessary. A person did not have to be charged with any crime, in a court of law, before being sent to jail.

The truth dawned on me, as it had undoubtedly dawned on many other Malawians, that our small impoverished nation had a monster which we could not control anymore. In the euphoria which followed our liberation from the shackles of colonialism, we had been conned into making Dr Hastings Kamuzu Banda our life-president. At first we had made him life-president of the political party, the Malawi Congress Party. Then we made him life-president of the nation.

We were told that it was necessary for the country to have political stability and economic development. The logic was simple. We were told that the only way to ensure political stability was to make Dr Banda our life-president. We swallowed it, hook, sink and all. He was a man of short-cuts. He never bothered to call for a referendum on the matter. He just got his MCP to pass a resolution and then Parliament was ordered to implement the wishes of "the People" by amending the constitution. Parliament did. In the final analysis we had very little of either political stability or economic development. Both were a chimera. All we definitely achieved was to place him beyond the reach of our censure. He was not subjected to the necessary ritual of elections any more. He could do with us as he pleased. There was precious little or nothing we could do about him. We had foolishly but collectively done away with our basic right to choose our own leaders. We had made ourselves politically impotent. He was too smart or cunning for us.

It is true that we had what looked like peace. But it was the peace of the cemetery. It was enforced silence which was mistaken for peace. Our lips were sealed by fear and death. Our pens were silenced by long jail terms, without trial.

It is true that we had what looked like political stability. But it was the kind of stability which is caused by overwhelming force.

When the thick boot is on the neck of a person who is prone on the ground, there can be no movement. The jails were full and murders were rampant. The murderers were above the law.

Instant death stalked any Malawian who dared to stray from the laid-down path. The victims ranged from ordinary villagers to sitting Cabinet Ministers. The death came in various forms. It did not matter whether you were in exile or at home. Sometimes it was instant death through a vicious clubbing down by members of the Youth League or Malawi Young Pioneers. Such a death was suffered by George Makwangwala who was District Chairman for Ntcheu of the same Malawi Congress Party which killed him. Sometimes it was instant death through a petrol bomb. Such a death was suffered by Mkwapatira Mhango, a Malawian journalist in exile in Lusaka, when his house was petrol-bombed at night and he perished, together with his two wives and eight children. Sometimes it was instant death from a bullet discharged from a gun in the hands of a hired assassin. Such a death was suffered by Dr Atati Mpakati, in a backstreet in Harare, after the poor man had survived a parcel-bomb. Sometimes it was death from an informal and secret, police assassination squad. Such a death was suffered by Cabinet Ministers Dick Matenje, Twaibu Sangala and Aaron Gadama, and Legislator David Chiwanga. Their deaths were announced as a road accident. And sometimes it was painful death through drowning in the Shire River, a form of death Banda fondly called "meat for crocodiles".

Churches were not exempted. When the Jehovah Witnesses refused to buy MCP membership cards by force, the church was proscribed, its property confiscated and its adherents run out of village and out of town. Those who were slow were mercilessly slaughtered and their corpses left in the forests to be eaten by hyenas. Those who were safe in exile in Zambia and Mozambique had their property either torched or given to MCP loyalists. Within one month the country had no single family belonging to the Jehovah Witnesses.

The world refused to believe this self-confessed murderer and continued to treat him with respect and honour as a wise statesman. The lenders poured money into Malawi to prop up his wicked and corrupt government. He was a staunch anti-communist, that is what mattered most. Nothing else did.

We had no economic development worth talking about, apart from his Press Corporation and the Lonrho Company of his personal and business friend, Tiny Rowland. Other investors were afraid of his Forfeiture Act. Male tourists did not like to go through a forced haircut at the airport. Female tourists did not like to endure the puritan dress-code which did not allow them to put on short dresses or slacks, regardless of the weather. A Malawian could make money only at considerable risk. After thirty years of independence, all the businesses of any significance were in the hands of foreigners, namely Asians and Whites. It was relatively safe for them to be seen to be rich. The Malawian was levelled through forced gifts, the Forfeiture Act and imprisonment without trial.

Dr Banda's stewardship of the affairs of the nation was not subject to the approval or disapproval of the electorate. He was beyond our control. He, in turn, had transformed a small department of the Malawi Police Force, the Special Branch, into another uncontrollable monster. The Special Branch became a law unto itself. It was neither accountable to the courts nor bound by any laws. The Special Branch had powers to lock up any Malawian, at any time, without any charge, and keep them indefinitely. They also had powers to kill in the course of their duty.

I was a civil servant in the super scale. I had risen relatively fast. I was twenty-nine years old and only six months married. My young wife was six months pregnant.

We had been watching her bulging tummy, proudly, month after month with a great deal of excitement. We wondered if our first-born was going to be a son or a daughter. She was certain that it was going to be a son. I was thinking the same but I was not so certain. What we were both certain of was the night she became pregnant. We had started counting the months from that day.

Little did I know that I would see my first-born son, for the first time, from inside a prison. When I saw him he was three-months-old and a grill separated us. I was a political prisoner of Dr Banda in Mikuyu Maximum Security Prison. I was not allowed to touch him, let alone carry or kiss him. My wife turned him around in her arms to face me. He looked at me and I looked at him through the wire mesh of the cage. The huge cage which separated us was made of hardwood and reinforced steel wire-mesh. It was so high and wide that a handshake across it was impossible. That was not enough. A stern-looking prison warder stood next to me to make sure that I was not left alone with my young family. His duty was to listen to every word of our conversation. His other duty was to ensure that my wife's visit did not exceed fifteen minutes.

I was dressed in a tattered prison uniform. The shorts had huge holes which exposed my buttocks. I had no problem with that because the cage was high enough and my wife could not see the shame there. The shirt was a different story. I borrowed one from a fellow prisoner because my own had huge holes which could have made my wife cry with shock. I was in a state of total degradation. Up until the day of my arrest, our marriage had been idyllic. We had been very deeply in love.

I had been seconded from the Ministry of Trade, Industry and Tourism, where I was Senior Trade Officer responsible for domestic trade, to the Office of the President and Cabinet. I was number two in the Viphya Pulp and Paper Corporation, a government-owned company. It had been incorporated a year before to exploit the vast pine forests on the Viphya Plateau, in the north of Malawi, for the production of pulp for the paper industry.

It was a vast project by Malawi standards. It was going to be the biggest the country had ever had. Total employment was going to be seven-thousand. Six-thousand of them were going to be involved in the logging operations in the forests. One-thousand people were going to be employed in three plants on the lakeshore area near Chintheche in Nkhata Bay. Jaako Poyry of Helsinki, Finland, were the consulting engineers.

The trees were going to be cut into logs and carried to the lakeshore by a fleet of large trucks. On arrival at the pulp-mill, the logs were going to be chipped, cooked and bleached into pulp. A separate plant was going to turn common salt into chlorine for the bleaching. The third plant was going to treat the used water from the pulp-mill before pumping it back into the lake to avoid pollution. Production was going to peak at five-hundred tonnes a day, all of which were going to be exported.

We had already sent a team to Chile in South America to study the use of oxen for the logging operations. We had also sent fourteen young men to Syracuse University in New York to study chemical, civil and mechanical engineering with a bias to wood-pulp technology. We had received a great deal of assistance from the United Nations Food and Agricultural Organisation (FAO). Everything was so smooth that we actually set 8 March 1978 as the day when we were going to press the button to set the huge rollers rolling. We set 8 June 1978 as the official opening day.

We had got a World Bank loan to build the Mazamba Road and another to modernize Chipoka Harbour. Barges were going to carry the bales of pulp from Chintheche to Chipoka and then cargo trains were going to carry the pulp to Nacala port in Mozambique.

My main area of responsibility was finance. I was the link between the corporation and prospective financial partners. The Chase Manhattan Bank in New York had already been identified to form and lead a syndicate of financiers.

We were about to sign on, officially, the technical and financial partners. My immediate superior was away in London with some members of the Board of Directors at that time. I was due to have a buffet dinner two days later with the Desk Officer for Malawi at the State Department in Washington. He had come all the way to learn something about the huge project which was going to transform the Malawi economy.

The morning after the dinner I was due to leave for Teheran in Iran with the late Dick Matenje, the Minister of Finance. We were going to receive a cheque for fifty-million dollars from the Shah of Iran as his contribution to the project. All he wanted was an opportunity to buy the pulp for the production of paper for use in an ambitious project he had for the expansion of education in his country.

That day I was on the third floor of Development House on Victoria Avenue in Blantyre where our offices were. I was busy supervising the carpeting of our offices by Press Furniture and Joinery. I was darting from door to door to ensure that the carpeting was done to my complete satisfaction.

At about ten o'clock in the morning, totally unexpectedly, a pot-bellied man appeared from the direction of the lift. He was dressed in a suit. The three men who followed him were shabbily dressed as if they were labourers looking for casual work for the day. He approached me in the corridor.

"Excuse me Sir," he said politely, "we are looking for Mr Mpasu."

"Do you know Mr Mpasu?" I asked him.

"No, I don't," he replied truthfully.

I wondered how any one could go out looking for a person they did not know except by name.

"I am Mr Mpasu," I told him innocently. He was taken aback but immediately composed himself.

"Can we see you in your office Sir?" he asked me.

"Sure," I said, "it is that door over there!"

Although I had pointed out the door to him, he stood still. He seemed extremely unwilling to enter my office ahead of me. Not wishing to inconvenience the visitors, I dropped everything I was doing in order to attend to them. I was sure that they would not stay long and I would resume my work immediately after they left.

As I walked towards the door of the office I noticed something strange. The shabbily dressed men flanked me on both sides. It was as if they were expecting me to run for safety and wanted to be at the ready to grab me.

When we entered my office all pretenses were immediately dispensed with. The last man closed the door behind him. He then leaned his back against it. No one else was to be allowed to enter my office. The other man went straight to the metal filing-cabinet at the corner. He pulled out the drawers one by one. He would pull out a suspicious looking file, flip through it and put it back. Sometimes he would go through the file so carefully and so slowly as if he was looking for a lost needle between the sheets.

The next man dashed for my desk. He too started to pull out the drawers. He seemed to be looking for a tiny postage stamp lost among the sheets.

It was very clear that they had taken over my office. I did not matter anymore. I was incensed. I just could not imagine how any one could be so rude as to behave like that and handle confidential documents in that matter. My patience ran out.

"Who are you?" I demanded

"I am Superintendent Mwanjasi from the Special Branch," the pot-bellied man replied very calmly.

"Can I see your identification please?" I demanded.

"I don't have any with me now. It does not matter anyway," he replied.

I told him that it mattered greatly to me, but he ignored me. That disarmed me completely. Here was a police officer with his men and none of them had any mark or item of identification! For all I knew these men could have been crooks out to filch company secrets.

"Can you show me your search warrant!" I demanded.

"What search warrant?" he replied to my question with ill-disguised contempt.

"What do you want?" I asked again.

"We have instructions to tell you that you are wanted at the Police Headquarters in Zomba," he replied.

Mr Kamwana was the Police Chief at that time, but I had no idea why he wanted to see me. Furthermore, I could not understand why he had not just phoned me up to fix an appointment. I would have driven to Zomba on my own without any hustles.

"If it is Mr Kamwana, tell him that I will see him tomorrow. I am busy today, as you can see," I said angrily.

"No! The orders are that we go with you. Orders are orders," he said emphatically.

"Is this an arrest?" I asked.

"No, it is not!" he replied untruthfully.

"Do you realise that you are killing off this huge project which was going to transform the Malawi economy?" I asked him indignantly.

"No man is indispensable. Even if you are not here tomorrow, there are others who will do the job," he replied arrogantly.

Here was this silly policeman totally unaware of the implications of his actions. I was fully convinced in my mind that if I was to be arrested all the financial partners were going to pull out of the project. Firstly, because, as their contact man, they would probably think that they had been dealing with a thief or an embezzler. Secondly, because, even if they would consider me innocent, the mere fact of arresting me would indicate to them a very high level of political insecurity which would expose their investment to unacceptable risks.

CHAPTER 2

Trip to Zomba Prison

To my surprise, they did not take any file or document from the office. However, one of them reached out for my Samsonite brief-case and ordered me to open it. I did. He rifled through whatever was in there until he came across a letter which my Ethiopian wife had written to her parents. The envelope was sealed. I had already affixed a postage stamp on it, ready to drop it in the post-office box. He picked up the envelope and tore it open to read the letter.

"What is this?" he asked me when he could not read the letter.

"It is written in Amharic, the Ethiopian official language," I replied.

"Read it to me!" he ordered.

"I can't," I replied.

He threw the letter back into the brief-case. I closed the brief-case and picked it up. They followed me out of the office, making sure that they flanked me on both sides. We walked along the corridor into the lift. As we came out of the lift on the ground floor, those who were waiting to catch the lift exchanged glances of surprise at the kind of company I was in. They hurriedly gave way to us.

Out on the street was a police car. The driver, the fifth man of the group, was the only one in police uniform. He opened the back door of the saloon for me to go in. I refused and started walking down towards my own private car. There was agitation. Two of them darted in front of me to cut me off. Their boss came over and confronted me.

"Why do you want us to use force on you, Sir? Would you like us to manhandle you in broad daylight, in a busy street like this, with everyone watching?" He tried to reason with me.

"There is no way I can leave my car on the street," I said with a degree of finality and defiance which surprised them.

I took out my car keys from my trousers pocket to open the car door. They surrounded me.

"Your car is safe here. We can look after it," he replied reassuringly.

"It is not safe and you know it is not safe," I said determinedly.

They were now at a loss. I offered them a compromise.

"If you think I am going to speed off and away, why don't you give me one of your men to come with me in my car?" I suggested.

The superintendent himself offered to come with me. He ordered his men to follow me in the police car. Their car followed mine. My house was in Namiwawa suburb on the road to Chilomoni. The kitchen window faced the road. My wife dropped whatever she was doing in the kitchen when she saw the police car, following my car into the garage, with all those strange men.

"What is it darling?" she asked worriedly when she opened the front door.

"I do not know," I replied. "These men say that I am wanted at the Police Headquarters in Zomba and I have come to leave the car here."

Without any excuse or an iota of politeness the strange men started searching the house. In the kitchen they dipped their fingers into a bag of rice and another of maize flour to feel if there was anything hidden there. They searched the larder thoroughly. In the sitting room they dipped their fingers into the cushions and the settees to feel whatever they were looking for. Then one of them went to the bookshelves to glance at the titles. He even checked for hidden things behind and between the books.

In the bedrooms it was worse. They felt the mattresses and pillows before they turned the mattresses over. Then they made a thorough search of the built-in wardrobes by feeling the clothes as well. In the bathroom it was absolutely comical. One of them lifted the lid of the cistern and dipped his hand into the water of the flush toilet. Afterwards, they gathered in the sitting room.

"What are you looking for?" I asked, exasperated.

"Anything dangerous!" was the instant reply.

11

"Is it perhaps this manuscript you are looking for?" I asked when I picked up a flat file on my bookshelf. They had seen it but had not recognised it.

When I was in Germany at the Malawi Embassy, I had spent many evenings writing a novel just to while away the time. I published the novel when I was transferred to the Malawi Embassy in Ethiopia. It was titled *Nobody's Friend*. I had heard a rumour that the Censorship Board had been uneasy about it. They thought that the title meant that Dr Banda, the life-president of Malawi, had no friends on the continent because of his bad policies. For that reason they were considering banning it. It just crossed my mind that perhaps the manuscript was what these policemen were looking for but did not want to tell me. They snatched the manuscript from me with amazing avidity as if it was the greatest treasure in the world.

"Let us go!" the superintendent said to me.

"Lunch is almost ready, darling," my wife said to me.

"He will be back very soon. Keep it on the table," the superintendent told her.

I was led into the back seat of the police car but then a thought crossed my mind. I asked the superintendent if I could speak with my wife alone. After some hesitation he allowed me. He had started to believe that I was not the type that bolts off. I walked towards my sobbing wife and whispered to her.

"I may not come back very soon, but I will. I do not trust these people. There seems to be something serious," I said.

I pulled out my cheque book and signed a cheque for her to draw out all the money I had in the bank, into cash.

"These people are known to freeze people's bank accounts and even forfeit them," I said to her. "Go and take out all the money as soon as possible. Buy an air-ticket and fly back to Ethiopia. I would like you to give birth in the presence of your mother otherwise you may suffer a lot here," I told her.

"Don't worry about me, darling," she said.

But I was very worried about her. In fact I thought she might miscarry because of the psychological strain.

They put me in the middle of the back seat with one policeman on one side and two policemen on the other, on a seat designed for three people only. The burly superintendent needed more room. He sat in front with the driver. They took me straight to the Southern Region Police Headquarters at Chichiri where their offices are. We ascended the stairs to the upper floor and headed for the back. They opened an office and asked me to sit down. Suddenly they became courteous towards me. They actually left me all alone in the office as they went for lunch.

After lunch they found me and asked if the people from Zomba had arrived.

"What people from Zomba?" I asked.

"The ones who are taking you to Zomba," they replied.

I was feeling hungry but there was nothing I could do. They had not allowed me to take lunch at my home. They had deceived my wife that I would actually return for my meal very soon. Now they went for lunch and left me without any meal. They did not even contemplate allowing me to venture out to buy a snack.

At about two o'clock in the afternoon, two familiar men walked into the office. They greeted me with a great deal of friendliness. I had known both men for many years.

One of them was Mazunda. He had been a school-mate of mine at Dedza Secondary School and a year-mate at Chancellor College of the University of Malawi. In fact we graduated together and received our degrees on the same day. He surprised everyone when he joined the Police Force after his university education. If my memory is correct, he was the first university graduate to join the Malawi Police Force. Many people did not expect him to survive for long. He did not, but that is beside the point.

The other familiar person was Charles Ngwata. Ever since I knew him he had always been in the Special Branch. He had been a regular visitor at Chancellor College to spy on students. Every dance we held at the college was sure to be attended by Ngwata. He spent most of his time at the bar drinking and listening to the idle talk of drunken students. He was always in plain clothes and ingratiated himself to several students. He was always pretty good

13

at pretending to be a trusted and sincere friend but never, never disclosed that he was a policeman.

Charles Ngwata and Mazunda asked me to go to Zomba with them. Outside the Police Station was an unmarked VW Kombi. The two of them sat in front. Mazunda drove the minibus. There was no tension in the car and we exchanged idle banter as old acquaintances.

At Njuli, Mazunda failed to control the car when a herd of goats darted across the road. He knocked down one of them killing it. The goat was pregnant. The owner was a woman. She went livid with obscenities and vituperation against Mazunda. Apologies were not acceptable. She demanded money for compensation and not for one but for several. Her goat, she said, had always given her two kid-goats every year. She absolutely refused to let the vehicle proceed any farther. The incident attracted public attention and more villagers came. None of them ever guessed they were dealing with policemen and the vehicle was a police vehicle.

A compromise was reached when I suggested that this was a road accident and the traffic police ought to be involved. She agreed to jump into the car on condition that she would be brought back. We drove to Namadzi Police Station where the matter was reported to the Traffic Police. Then we drove back to Njuli with the Traffic Constables who took measurements at the scene of the accident. We left the woman there with the assurance that the question of compensation for her dead goat was now in the hands of the traffic police.

Back at Namadzi we dropped the traffic constables and proceeded to Zomba. When we approached Zomba Central Prison, almost as an afterthought, Ngwata asked Mazunda to drive through the prison fence because he wanted to see someone else briefly. Then he turned to me with a smile. He asked me if I minded a brief stop. I said I did not mind. He then drove right up to the prison gate itself.

Ngwata got out of the vehicle and used his right fist to bang on the metal prison-door. He hit it incessantly until it was opened from inside. Ngwata pulled out a piece of paper from the inside pocket of his jacket. He handed it over to the prison warder who had opened the door.

"Keep this one for us. We shall come for him!" he said and pointed at me.

I was so shocked. I did not believe what I heard. Me, in prison? He ordered me out of the vehicle into the prison. Sure enough, the piece of paper he had handed over was a warrant for my imprisonment. The huge, metal door closed behind me. The two policemen drove away.

CHAPTER 3

A Little Bit About Me

I was born on 17 September 1945 in a rural setting. I was born and brought up in Khuzi Village, in Chief Kwataine's area, in Ntcheu District.

For the first five years of my life I was the only child. The earliest impression I had of my father was from his portrait on the wall of our living room and from his bicycle and Singer sewing machine. He was working in South Africa.

My mother was the person I knew closely and lived with. She was the youngest of three sisters in a family of seven children. My maternal grandparents were alive and well. They were very fond of me. I had many cousins and cross-cousins to play with, apart from other numerous playmates in the village. My maternal grandmother, Rebecca Khuzi, was the eldest daughter of the Chief of the village. My maternal grandfather, Mwachande Kanzangaza, was the eldest son of another Chief of Kanzangaza Village. What I still remember, with a great deal of fondness, was that he had a large herd of cattle and made sure that my breakfast of maize-flour porridge was cooked, not with water, but with fresh milk every day. We were great friends. I remember once I made him laugh uproariously when I asked a barber to give me a haircut like his. I thought that his bald head was a special haircut. Another day, after Sunday school, I asked him a very difficult question which he failed to answer. I asked him that if God had created everything and everybody, then who had created God? He referred me back to the missionaries.

My paternal grandfather, Lemoth Mpasu, was also alive. He was a senior man in a breakaway African Christian Church. He, too, had a large herd of cattle. He had a shop in the village where people bought their requirements and where his tailors patched up

16

the people's torn clothes. I never saw my paternal grandmother, as she died the year I was born. She was nee Bertha Chawanje. Her father founded and became Chief of two villages: Chawanje Village in Soche and Chawanje Village near Lunzu, both in Blantyre.

Both sides of my family were Ngoni. They had entered Malawi through that part of Mozambique known as Angonia Province where they had originally settled on their way from South Africa. In fact, quite regularly, members of the two families who had remained in Mozambique were visitors to our village but I was never able to cross over into Mozambique and see them. There is now, I regret to say, a complete break between the families. We do not know them any more.

When I was about three-years-old, one day, a strange man came to our house at dusk. He had a brand new, small suitcase with him. My mother received him. He disclosed that he had been working with my father in Cape Town, South Africa and, on his return, my father had sent a parcel for me which he came to deliver. I was very excited to hear my name from the lips of the strange man. Indeed, the small suitcase was mine. It was full of my clothes. I remember a child's suit, a cap and a pair of black leather shoes. I went over the moon with happiness.

A year later, also at dusk, another strange man arrived followed by porters who carried two large trunks. Instantly our living room was filled with well-wishers to greet the strange man. He was my father. We became instant friends. He won me over with lots of nice things which he gave me. He also started carrying me on his bicycle and even allowed me to play with it on my own. A year after his arrival my sister was born. Two years after that my brother was born.

When I was five years old, my father took me to the village mission school to be enrolled. The teacher ordered me to touch the left ear-lobe with my right hand directly across my head. My fingers could not reach the ear-lobe. He said I was too young to start school and sent me away. My father was adamant. He pleaded with him. The only concession the teacher made was to

17

allow me to play with his pupils during their break-time but never to enter the class. I took advantage of that privilege.

The following year my fingers could touch the ear-lobe. I was enrolled in sub-standard one. At the end of the year I came first in my class but did not tell my parents because I had gone straight from school to play with my playmates near the river. The teacher himself told my father. He said it in such a way that my father became visibly alarmed that he would not be able to educate me fully if he did not have a credible source of regular income in the village.

My father made preparations to return to South Africa. On the morning of his departure he set aside some documents on the verandah of our house. Then he lit a match to another set of documents he wanted destroyed. When he entered the house to get his jacket, I stoked the dying flames and put the documents he had set safely aside on the fire. When he came out he was aghast.

"What are you doing?" he asked angrily.

"I am helping you to burn the papers," I replied innocently, pleased with myself at the valuable assistance I was rendering my dear father.

He smiled at me and went back into the house. Neighbours told him that he was lucky because his ancestral spirits, through me, had stopped him from going away.

Little did I realise that I had burnt his travel documents. His trip was over before it had started. He could not go to his old job in South Africa anymore.

It was almost a year later when he managed to arrange for another trip to Southern Rhodesia, now Zimbabwe, to look for a job. Within a few months of his arrival there he arranged for my mother, my sister and my brother to go and join him. But not me. He wrote me a very nice letter to say that he wanted me to be educated here, not there. I was left in the hands of my two aunts and maternal grandparents. He was working for the Water Development in charge of water-pumping stations. He worked in Gatooma, Marandellas and other places but stayed long at Norton.

My third year of schooling was at Malonda Junior Primary

School, another mission school which was several miles away. The daily walk was a strain. When my mother came on home leave she was appalled to see the distance I was covering daily on foot. She made a strong appeal to my father for a bicycle. His old bicycle had ceased to exist. He immediately sent me a brand new bicycle. The following year the whole family came on home leave. He brought me another bicycle. With two bicycles to myself, life was a lot easier than before. I began to enjoy school.

By some strange coincidence a new teacher came to our school. He was from Mchinji. He was unmarried and a Catholic, while our school was Protestant. His name was Africano Sumaili. It was he who really made me love school. He had a totally different approach to teaching youngsters. He never scowled or whipped anyone. He spoke to us like to grown-up people. He inspired us with lofty sentiments and encouragement. As a result, we were too ashamed to do anything stupid. Our class was the best in everything. We were the neatest and best behaved. Our knowledge of English and Arithmetic, including Mental Arithmetic, was better than that of the class above us. At the end of the year he asked the Head-Teacher to set the examinations and invigilate us. The whole class passed. The lowest had 60%. The Head-Teacher was furious. He decided to give us an English dictation by reading a passage rather fast. Five got below 50%. He made them repeat the class while the rest of us went to the next class. Mr Africano Sumaili was too good to last. He had made many enemies because of his success and left. As for me the change had already been made. He made me fall in love with the quest for knowledge.

My class was the first to start senior primary school at Malonda. Our teacher was the late Roy Kaenda. In 1960 I wrote the Primary School Leaving Certificate Examinations. I came first and was accepted for Form One at Dedza Secondary School in 1961. I have a feeling that Dedza moulded my character. It was a school that allowed a student to develop himself in a competitive atmosphere. It gave each student a very high degree of self-confidence and, to some extent, initiative and leadership skills. I was not outstanding in sports or games, but at one time or another I was chairman of the Current Affairs Society, the Debating Society, the Mechanical Society, the Photographic Society and the Geographical Society. I was also on the editorial board of the school magazine *Sapere Aude*, Latin for "dare to be wise".

I wrote my Cambridge School Certificate Ordinary Level Examination in November 1964. In 1965, I was one of the one-hundred students who started the University of Malawi at Chancellor College in Blantyre. I took Philosophy, Psychology, Sociology, History, English and Biology, but I eventually fell in love with Economics and English Literature, in which I majored. Dr Hastings Kamuzu Banda, the country's first and only Prime Minister, was then in the process of building up his single-party dictatorship. He was rather nervous about everything. The previous year, 1964, he had a traumatic experience when six of his eight Cabinet Ministers fell out with him. The incident caused a serious security situation. It made him very unpopular with the educated and urban masses. He was undeterred and was busy passing draconian laws through a Parliament that was virtually handpicked.

At the end of my first year at Chancellor College, I understand I was the best student in English. I never proved it though. I spent the holiday earning extra money as District Census Supervisor in Ntcheu. When I reported for the second year at the end of September 1966, I was pleasantly surprised to learn from Dr Ian Michael, the Vice Chancellor, that I had been awarded a Student Leadership Travel grant by the United States government to visit the USA for six weeks, all expenses paid. It was a unique, once-in-a-lifetime opportunity. There were fifteen of us from around the world. I was the only black and the others came from Denmark, Austria, Luxembourg, Yugoslavia, Bolivia, Japan, Ecuador, Laos, Cambodia, Thailand and Morocco.

In fact I was late by one week. My colleagues had started the programme in Washington. I joined them in New York. Nelson Rockefeller, the late billionaire, was running for Governor of New York. We went to his campaign headquarters to meet him.

We had visits and discussions with fellow students and faculty in several universities in and around New York. The burning issues in American politics at that time were the Vietnam War and the civil rights of American blacks. It was embarrassing sometimes when I was mistaken for an American black. President Lyndon Johnson was having a tough time over the Vietnam War.

After a few days in New York, we caught a Greyhound bus for Massachusetts. We were hosted by Amherst College which is an outstanding college for the sons of the well-to-do. My host was George Damon. He was driving a beautiful Volvo car. To me the idea that a student could own and drive a car was eye-popping. He told me that they had three cars in their family. Another thing I found strange at Amherst was the fact that fresh milk was completely free in the cafeterias, just like drinking water.

While at Amherst College, we drove over, for discussions to Mt Holyoake College and Smith College, both of which are upper class colleges for girls. We also had discussions with the students at the universities of Massachusetts, Boston, and Harvard. We were even allowed to attend some lectures.

After a few days, we caught a plane to Atlanta in Georgia. A certain Lester Maddox was running for Governor of Georgia. Maddox's claim to fame, in fact the *raison d'etre* of his whole campaign, was the fact that he had personally used an axe-handle to chase away blacks from his restaurant. Maddox eventually won the election on a racist ticket but after a tie and a re-run. While in Atlanta we were given a chance to spend a whole day at the offices of the biggest newspaper. We also visited the world headquarters of the Coca-Cola Company.

What was not on the programme was the Ku Klux Klan. I leaned on my hosts to arrange a meeting for me to meet the Ku Klux Klan. They were embarrassed but I insisted. They got me to see a lawyer who regularly defended the Ku Klux Klan and was widely assumed to be one of them. I asked him what he thought was wrong with blacks. His argument was that blacks had no reason to be in America and should go back to Africa. I asked him why he himself did not go back to Europe where his ancestors had come from. He said he could not because the white man was in America to civilize the Red Indians. I asked him which Red Indian tribe had entrusted the white man with such a mission to civilize them. He said it was a God-given mission. As a debater, he was a dead loss. I wondered how he won cases in the courts defending the Ku Klux Klan.

The same thing happened to Lester Maddox when I met him at a breakfast meeting. His prepared speech was all racist. He was at a loss when he saw me, a black, in a group he had expected to be entirely white. I really enjoyed his discomfiture as he tried to skip some of the offensive words in the speech in order to spare me the embarrassment.

After Atlanta we flew to Dallas in Texas. There was sensational news created by a man who had gone to a beauty salon. There he had ordered all the women to lie face down on the floor and shot them dead, one by one. Only a baby was spared. What I never understood was why the women never scrambled for safety after the first shots. Apparently everyone waited for her bullet. It was a grisly but senseless massacre.

Next we flew to Albuquerque and Santa Fe in New Mexico. We stayed with host families. My hosts for a week were a retired couple Mr and Mrs Diehl. I had a memorable day in the reserve with Navajo Indians. They have a very rich culture. New Mexico is a crucible where Indian, Spanish and other European cultures mixed. One special treat the US government gave us was a rare visit to Los Alamos Laboratories, deep in the pine forests of the mountains. It was a rare privilege and honour. Los Alamos Laboratories is where they made the Hiroshima and Nagasaki bombs. We were shown the models. Los Alamos is a self-contained, restricted community of highly trained scientists, many of them with more than two doctorates. The scale of their salaries was obviously high because many of them had private aeroplanes parked in front of their houses.

The next stage was Boulder in Colorado where I saw snow for the first time in my life. We stayed with the students at the university in their hostels. What I remember about this leg of the trip was a nasty trick that was played on me by a friend from Finland. He was at the University on a Rotary Club scholarship. I had dressed casually that day, in a skipper, believing that the day was free. He came from nowhere, almost breathless. He said he had been looking for me all over the campus and could I please accompany him to a Rotary Club lunch meeting. I agreed, but he refused to let me go and dress up. We have no time, he said, in any case Americans are informal. Foolishly I believed him. We drove over to the hotel where the function was being held.

To my horror it was not an ordinary Rotary Club lunch meeting. The guest speaker was an eminent physicist who was due to talk about possible military uses of laser-beams. He talked about laser-beams powerful enough to cut flying aeroplanes in half. Before everything started, my Finnish friend excused himself, but returned a short time later. When the formalities began, the president began announcing the names of visitors. I thought I was safe. I was not. He announced my name last. I had to stand up, dressed casually in a skipper like that, in a room that was full of well-dressed Congressmen, Senators, professors and business executives. I was about to sit down gratefully, believing that it was all over, when the president said: "Mr Mpasu will address us!" He immediately left the podium and the lectern with all its microphones. The television cameras zoomed in on me. There was no where for me to hide and no where to flee to. My Finnish friend was mischievously beside himself with glee. I walked, like a condemned man to his fate, and ascended the podium. I faced the microphones. On the spur of the moment I decided to talk about myself, my country and why I was in the United States. When I ended, there was a thunderous applause. Many of those bigshots stepped forward to shake my hand. My Finnish friend was immensely pleased with himself although I thought that my humiliation was complete. We joked about it many times afterwards. He said he knew I could do it and wanted the Americans to know something about Africa and Malawi.

After Colorado we flew to San Francisco in California. We stayed at Berkeley College. A certain Ronald Reagan, an actor, had announced his intention to run for Governor of California. He made a single promise to the voters. He said that his first act in office, if elected, would be to sack the Vice Chancellor of the University of Southern California in order to get the troublesome university students back into the lecture-rooms. He blamed campus unrest on weak administration by the Vice Chancellor. He won the elections. The Vice Chancellor resigned before he could be fired. He too went into politics, ran for the US Senate and won.

It was very exciting for our group of young men and women to meet some of these people as early as 1966, long before they had made it to the US presidency and Congress. *Time* magazine interviewed us. It wrote a feature story with our faces in art form on its cover. We were called the under-twenty-five future leaders of the world.

We flew to Washington for debriefing and then dispersed. I decided to return to Malawi via London. I had a whole day there just roaming about. I made sure to visit Trafalgar Square and No. 10 Downing Street where I had my picture taken.

On return to Malawi I had to face the reality that I had missed five weeks of lectures and study. My friends lent me their lecture notes. I applied myself very hard just to catch up.

When the Christmas holiday approached, two of my friends, James Munthali and Chadwick Mphande, and I decided to spend it in Zambia where we had relatives. We caught a night bus in Blantyre which arrived in Lilongwe in the early morning. Someone sneaked out to Lilongwe Police Station to report that three prominent "rebels", Henry Chipembere, Orton Chirwa and Kanyama Chiume, were in town and had just jumped off the Blantyre bus.

I was mistaken for Henry Chipembere, Chadwick Mphande was mistaken for Orton Chirwa and James Munthali was mistaken for Kanyama Chiume. The police immediately fetched their guns and got into a landrover to go and capture the "rebels". When they reached Lilongwe bus depot, they learned that the"rebels" had just boarded the bus for Lusaka in Zambia. This piece of news confirmed their worst fears. The landrover chased the bus until they caught up with it on the Mchinji road. Fortunately, the police knew better and had their own doubts. When the bus stopped at a stage I was the first to get out. I wanted to buy a cold drink in a roadside grocery shop. When they saw me they concluded that it was all a question of mistaken identity. I was much too young to be mistaken for Henry Chipembere. They returned quietly without causing any incident. We continued our trip to Zambia without the slightest worry.

The second term opened in January 1967. Dr Banda was no longer Prime Minister, but President. A friend of mine, John Phiri, was the chairman of the debating society. He asked me to be the main speaker against a motion on the Single-Party State System in a debate with cabinet ministers and Malawi Congress Party functionaries. I agreed. We all looked forward to having great fun with the Malawi Congress Party heavyweights such as Albert Muwalo, Aleke Banda and possibly John Msonthi, purely as an academic or intellectual exercise. They chickened out. Dr Banda did not want his ministers humiliated by mere students.

When the third term opened, the entire committee of the Debating Society, together with the Catering Committee, were expelled summarily by Dr Banda personally.

The real surprise was me. I had no idea why he expelled me as well. The hand-written note he had sent to John Msonthi, who was the Chairman of the University Council, put my name at the top. He had written my first name five times and my surname three times to cover all possible spelling mistakes. He wrote: Samuel, Samwele, Samuele, Samule or Samuyele, Mpasu, Mpaso or Mphaso. Mr Msonthi gave me the note to read for myself. To me it indicated that Dr Banda was determined to ensure that I was definitely expelled from the university.

When elections were held to the Students' Union, I was away in America. Consequently, I held no position in any committee of the Students' Union. But here I was being expelled as the ringleader of the troublesome students. John Msonthi was very disappointed but there was very little he could do to defend us.

Rumours pointed at Albert Muwalo and Aleke Banda as the two ministers who had pressed for our expulsions.

Expulsions were not enough. Dr Banda called for an extraordinary two-day convention of his Malawi Congress Party at Kwacha Conference Centre in Blantyre to publicly denounce us. The District Committee of the Malawi Congress Party in Kasungu, Dr Banda's home district, also held a convention and immediately passed a resolution that all of us, troublesome and ungrateful students, should be sent to the notorious Dzeleka Detention Camp to be cured of our ingratitude. We were eight in total: Samuel Mpasu, John Phiri, Isaac Vareta, Justin Thundu, Crispin Ng'oma, Hanleck Ngoma, Suzgo Munthali and Manuel Mwimba. Fortunately, Dr Banda did not get the popular endorsement to detain us which he had expected to get at the Kwacha Conference Centre.

For some strange reason, I decided to write to Dr Banda personally for an explanation. He never replied. When the annual convention of the Malawi Congress Party was held in Mzuzu in September the same year, Dr Banda climbed down. He personally ordered that all the expelled students should go back to the university. I was glad to go back. I had just gone through a very bad time.

I had been shadowed for days on end. I had lived in constant fear of getting killed, day after day, week after week and month after month. The announcement allowing us to go back to the university lifted off the burden of fear from my mind. From 7 May to 17 September 1967 my life had been a daily nightmare.

Our return to college did not please everyone. The students who were police informants and Malawi Congress Party loyalists were very disappointed. There was division in the University Senate and University Council as well. Some of them wanted us to repeat the second year but the others wanted us to proceed into the third year. A compromise was reached. We were given three weeks to prepare and write the year-end examinations of the second year. If we passed we would proceed into the third year. If we failed we would be relegated to the second year to repeat it. We spent sleepless nights. Fortunately, we all passed.

The political friction between the Malawi Congress Party and the university did not diminish. *Malawi News*, the party's newspaper, and the Malawi Broadcasting Corporation regularly carried denunciations of us students. Many of us came to believe that Dr Banda would not bother to expel students any more but would just close down the entire university and get done with it.

Another friend, the late Ted Mwaya, approached me with a nomination form one day. He begged me to run for the chairmanship of the Students' Union. Chimwemwe Hara's term of office as Chairman of the Students' Union was coming to an end amid chaos.

"You have suffered already and would not like to suffer again," Ted said. "Please save the university otherwise these people will close it down. I want to complete my degree course."

I signed the nomination form just to please Ted. My aim was to withdraw my candidature just before the voting. Unknown to me, Ted took the nomination form I had signed to show to each of the other candidates. He intimidated them that they had no chance in the elections against me. They withdrew before I did. Much against my own wishes, I found myself elected the new Chairman of the Students' Union, unopposed. I could not be called President because that was reserved for Dr Banda by the Malawi constitution.

During my term of office the level of denunciation by the Malawi Congress Party went down a bit. Initially all my friends told me I was crazy to go into student politics after the suffering I had just gone through. My own view was that if I had suffered so much without going into student politics then I might as well go into student politics. It was better for me to suffer for my own mistakes rather than suffer again because of mistakes which were going to be made by others. I went ahead and got the Polytechnic, Bunda College of Agriculture, Soche Hill Teachers Training College and Mpemba School of Public Administration into a University Students' Union. I was simultaneously chairman of our College Union and the University Union.

I graduated on 24 July 1969. I received my degree certificate from the hands of the same Dr Banda who had expelled and re-admitted me. He was the university Chancellor.

I had several job offers before I graduated. I chose one which offered me more money and the quickest promotion prospects. It was Horace Hickling and Company, a trading company with its headquarters in Britain. I was mistaken. The plan was that I was going to be a Management Trainee for six months, become the Commercial Manager after that and then replace the General Manager after four years.

The snag was that the Commercial Manager was not anxious to go back to Britain. He loved Malawi very much. He made my life hell as soon as the General Manager went on home leave. I have never met a racist like that one. He never allowed me to receive or make a telephone call. He hid the files from me as well. In the end he took me out of the office and put me at the reception to receive customers. At lunch hour he drove home but locked the building to leave us outside in the open, even when it was soaking rain.

After the end of my six months training period, I told the General Manager that his Commercial Manager needed the job more than I did. I left. My nasty experience at that company was news all over Malawi. It was given as an example in Parliament of how Africanisation was being resisted in the private sector. I was surprised when I was immediately offered a job in the Ministry of Trade, Industry and Tourism to be the man responsible for promoting and encouraging industrial investment in Malawi.

In my new post, I wielded so much influence that I could have easily got the racist man deported. I did not. I enjoyed the discomfort he experienced whenever we accidentally bumped into each other. One day, I walked into Kandodo Supermarket in Blantyre only to see him race through the back, leaving all the shopping to his wife. The company fired him anyway. He had embarrassed it. He left Malawi earlier than he had expected.

After fifteen months in the Ministry of Trade, Industry and Tourism, I was appointed into the diplomatic service. This was another surprise. I was made Second Secretary (Commercial) at the Malawi Embassy in Bonn. I had a wonderful time in Germany after I had learnt a bit of the language. After fifteen months I was posted to the Malawi Embassy in Addis Ababa, Ethiopia, where I met my future wife. After ten months in Addis Ababa I was promoted to Senior Trade Officer responsible for domestic trade. I returned to Malawi to take up the post. After five months in that post, I was seconded to the Viphya Pulp and Paper Corporation soon after it had been incorporated. Exactly twelve months later, the five policemen from the Special Branch collected me from the offices of that company.

Perhaps a word about my marriage. I had never been serious about marriage all along, perhaps because I never really had problems getting girlfriends. Between love and sex, I chose sex. I was more devoted to my job than to love affairs. It never occurred to me that some of the young women were serious about me and that I was breaking their hearts. While I was in the Viphya Pulp and Paper Corporation, a certain young lady who was my girlfriend came home one Sunday morning. She sneaked into my kitchen and started to put a black powder into a pot of chicken on the electric stove which my cook was preparing for me. As she tapped the powder into the pot, she murmured incantations. My cook caught her red-handed in the act as he returned from the servants' quarters. His shoeless feet did not make noise on the cement floor. That incident shook me up thoroughly. It was a love potion. My cook's fortuitous return saved me. The girl fled in shame. The chicken was thrown away. That was when I decided to get married, but to the girl-friend I had left behind in Addis Ababa. I sent her a return air-ticket. We got married at the Registrar General's office in Blantyre. Six months later, the Special Branch got me.

CHAPTER 4

The Interrogation

When the large, metal door of Zomba Central Prison closed with a bang behind me, I came face to face with the prison warders. They seemed too busy to attend to me so I sat down on a form. It seemed to me that good manners were out of place.

"Sit down on the floor!" one of them shouted at me very angrily. "A prisoner does not sit on a chair!" he added.

It did not make sense to me that I should sit down on the floor while there were unoccupied chairs in the office. Nevertheless, although dressed in a suit, I sat down on the floor. I was simmering with rage at my humiliation and helplessness.

At last one of them took out a blank, red folder and started to take down my personal details of name, village, date of birth, next of kin and so forth. Then I was ordered to empty all my pockets, take off my wrist-watch and wedding-ring. I surrendered all to him. Then he demanded my tie, belt, shoes and socks as well. He shoved all of these into a cloth bag which he tossed at the corner of the office. He was through with me.

I was taken out of the administration block into the courtyard. We immediately turned right. The next block served as a clinic on top but underneath were three cells. The prison warder opened the middle cell and pushed me in. He closed the door and bolted it from outside. It was a bare, empty cell. A few minutes later, the door opened again. The guard tossed an old threadbare blanket at me. I caught it with my hands before it could fall on the floor. He looked at me with contempt as if I was not worth speaking to. As far as he was concerned, I was probably less than human or an animal.

He walked away without saying a word. His colleague, who carried a gun, closed the door and then stood guard outside. He used a peep-hole to check on me regularly. I wondered if they would spare the life of that warder if by any chance I escaped. It seemed to me that they, too, were prisoners of a sort. They had to do what they were doing even if they hated it.

The thought of escape was utterly unrealistic. The walls were very thick. The door itself was thick and made of hardwood. There was a tiny window at the top but it was full of thick, steel bars. Besides, the window itself was so high that one would need a ladder to reach it. And it was on the same side where the guard stood. The ceiling was the concrete floor of the upper storey. There was no lighting. Digging the floor was impossible with bare hands. It was concrete.

My threadbare blanket was more than a blanket. It was a bed, a mattress, a bedsheet and a blanket, all rolled into one. It was the only thing between me and the bare concrete floor. I was so bewildered that I could not believe or understand what was happening to me. Luckily, the weather in January was fairly warm, but I dreaded what it was like in June when the temperatures dropped.

I spread the blanket on the bare floor. I lay down. I folded my jacket to use it as a pillow. I blinked wide awake for a good part of the night wondering what was happening to me. I was very worried about my wife and her delicate condition. I had not eaten anything the whole day yet they had locked me up for the night without giving me a glass of water or a morsel of food.

It was a long, long night. Morning broke in the end. I heard the sound of keys in the padlock and then the bolt being pulled back. The door was opened to check if I was still in. For some strange reason they kept the door open this time. Later on they allowed me to step outside if I wanted to, but not much farther than the doorstep. The armed guard was trying to be friendly as soon as he ensured that none of his colleagues was looking at him. I sat on the doorstep.

"Is it possible for me to go to the toilet, wherever it is?" I asked him.

"Let us go. I will escort you," he replied. "But you must not speak with anyone."

With his gun on the shoulder he came behind me. He stood by as I faced the urinal. The thought of walking barefoot in that busy toilet, which was hardly clean, filled me with fear about contracting all sorts of diseases.

On return to my cell we found an old prisoner with a wizened, weather-beaten face and a head which was entirely covered with grey hair, waiting for me. He had brought me an old, badly dented, aluminium plate, half-full of porridge. He looked at me with understanding. He shook his head in dismay.

"Eat!" he said. "Prison food is not anything like home food, but that is the only way to stay alive here."

"Where is the spoon and the sugar?" I asked him in all sincerity.

"Sugar and a spoon, in prison?" he asked me, in total disbelief over my naivety.

He laughed a little. He then demonstrated how I could eat the porridge. Eating on a table while sitting on a chair was a luxury that was not available. I sat on the floor.

I lifted the plate to my lips with both hands. I sucked the porridge into my mouth a little at a time. He watched me excitedly as if he was watching a child who was beginning to walk. He displayed a big smile after I had finished.

"Do not be disheartened, this is what men must sometimes go through in life," he told me encouragingly.

"Why am I not allowed to speak to you or to anyone?" I asked.

"That is nonsense. Do not bother about them," he said nonchalantly. "They are trying to intimidate you."

I was really glad to have someone to talk to. At least someone who was not afraid of the arbitrary rules. Apparently, they had appointed him to look after me as a way of preventing me from meeting the other prisoners. He brought me food from the kitchen every day and took back the plate. They did not want me to move away from my cell.

"What are you in prison for?" I asked him.

"Theft," he said quite happily, as if theft was something to be proud of.

"How long have you been here and when are you getting released?" I asked him again.

He laughed a bellyful.

"You see," he said, "they built this prison in 1938 and that was the first time I came in. I built it. I have been here ever since."

This was 1975. I could not believe that the man had been in this horrible place for 37 years.

"Are you here for murder perhaps?" I asked him.

"No, no. The only crime I know is theft," he replied honestly.

"You see, when they first locked me up, I was young. After my sentence I went home but I felt out of place. I had no family and no friends. They all felt ashamed of me. They kept away from me. So I stole again in order to come back. This is my home now. I will die here. Whenever my sentence is over, I reserve my place in the cell. I get back the same day. All I do is pick somebody's pocket at the bus station in full view of a policeman. Sometimes I just snatch a banana from a baby's hand and if it cries then that is it; I run a little to allow the people to catch me. When they take me to the police station, I know I am back in prison. The only regret I have is that such small thefts do not get me many years of imprisonment," he said with a straight face.

I could not believe what this old man was saying. One day in that place was too long for me. Yet he wanted to spend the rest of his life there.

"When they let you out, why don't you get a job?" I asked him. "And look after myself?" he asked me as an answer. Then he laughed. "I tried that once but got bored with waiting for my pay-day. I stole my employer's wrist-watch in order to come back here."

"Don't you feel like having a wife and children? Having a family you can really be proud of?" I asked him.

"What can I give to a family?" he replied.

I got the impression that life had no real meaning to the man. His permanent stay in prison was all that life meant to him.

He disappeared at two o'clock in the afternoon and brought me a plate of badly cooked *nsima* and a metal mug half-full of badly cooked pegion peas. That was both my lunch and dinner. The food was very unpalatable, but he encouraged me to eat it in order to preserve my life. At four o'clock in the afternoon I was ordered back into my cell. The door was bolted from outside and locked.

When they opened my cell again in the morning I was surprised to see a white man sitting on the doorsteps of the next cell. He, too, was completely bewildered. I gathered a little bit of courage to defy the orders. I greeted the white man in the presence of the prison guard. We got talking. The guard ignored us. The only thing the white man could not stomach was the terrible food. He refused to touch it. He told them that he was prepared to die from starvation. They buckled down and brought him half a loaf of bread and a small can of sardines. His problem was how to eat that bounty without the aid of a table knife, a fork or a spoon. But he soon overcame that by using his unwashed fingers.

Apparently his crime was that he had made some remarks about the political situation in the country when one of his employees was picked up by the Special Branch. Without checking out the veracity of the allegation he was pulled out of his car and rushed to Zomba prison in a police car. That was his arrest, trial, conviction and sentence. That morning he was making a great deal of fuss about the need to see his ambassador urgently. He was a South African and a General Manager of a company in Blantyre. In the afternoon his ambassador, accompanied by his wife, arrived to see him. Later in the evening the police came to take him out. I learnt that he was deported out of the country on twenty-four hours notice.

On Friday morning, I was on my way to the common toilet when a sick man called my name out from the balcony of the upper storey which served as a clinic.

"Hey Sam, it's me Richard. Richard Sembereka!"

The name did not fit the appearance of the man. I was horrified with what I saw. I had known Richard Sembereka for many years. The last time I had seen him he was the Minister of Labour, a plump and well-dressed man. That was several years before but here was a pathetic-looking skeleton of a man, completely disfigured and destroyed by his long imprisonment. My eyes welled up with tears as I desperately tried to take in the entire picture. The unanswered question I asked myself in my mind was, if this cruel and beastly government could do that to its own Cabinet Minister, then how much more would it do to me, a humble civil servant.

According to the story which circulated at the time Mr Richard Sembereka disappeared, he had been driving in his ministerial black Mercedes Benz car from Zomba to Blantyre, with the pennant flying on the bonnet, when the police stopped the car at a road-block. Without much ceremony the police pulled him out of the ministerial car and shoved him into a waiting police vehicle. He was then driven straight to Zomba prison for his long, indefinite imprisonment without charge or trial. Five or so years on, he had been reduced to this pathetic skeleton in front of my eyes. I think he saw the distress in my eyes and read my mind.

"Steel yourself up," he said, "it is a very tough world!"

I waved my hand feebly at him, but the prison guard pushed me on. We continued to the public toilet.

On return from the toilet, I was called out to the administration block. Charles Ngwata had come for me. I was led out of the prison to a waiting small van. I was told to go into the back of that van. He closed the door from outside and turned to join the driver in the cab. There were no seats in the van. I sat on the floor.

On arrival at Zomba Police Headquarters, I was led to the Special Branch offices which were in a two-storey block on its own. We climbed stairs to the upper storey where the office of Focus Gwede was. He was not in. I was made to wait in an adjoining office. What I immediately noticed was the atmosphere of fear and trepidation which pervaded the whole place. The policemen could not even mention the name of Focus Gwede but referred to him reverently as "Bwana". He was obviously something of a small god around there. On the grass lawn outside sat small groups of men, women and children, waiting fearfully for this small god to give them permits to visit their relatives in Zomba and Mikuyu prisons.

Focus Gwede was Deputy Head of the Special Branch at the time but he behaved very much as if he owned the place entirely. His close association with Albert Muwalo, who was both the Secretary General and Administrative Secretary of the Malawi Congress Party, ensured that he wielded a lot of power. Mr Muwalo was virtually Home Affairs Minister, although none of that was reflected in his job title. Pretty soon, the Head of the Special Branch, Mr Kumpukwe, was appointed into the Diplomatic Service and posted to Britain. Focus Gwede then formally took over as Head of the Special Branch.

A poor messenger was getting out of Gwede's office where he had gone to leave files. He was spotted by none other than Gwede himself. Gwede came up the stairs seething and trembling with rage. He went straight for the poor messenger. Gwede repeatedly and threateningly jabbed his right-hand forefinger on the messenger's chest.

"You do not enter my office when I am not there! Do you understand?" shouted Gwede repeatedly in his rage.

"Yes Sir! No Sir! I am sorry Sir! I will not do it again Sir!" whined the poor messenger subserviently.

He was expecting the whole world to explode in his face any moment.

I watched the whole incident with disgust. I do not know if the incident was stage-managed by Gwede for effect on me and the others. If it was, then it certainly lowered my opinion of Gwede in my mind. I had known Gwede before for some years. I had never known him or even imagined him to be such a mean-spirited terror. If a messenger in full police uniform could not enter Gwede's office, then why on earth was the office left open and why didn't Gwede clean his own office?

Anyway, Gwede cooled down. The poor messenger gratefully walked away, thankful that his explanations and apologies had been accepted. The fact that he had been humiliated in public counted for nothing. I could not understand why he did not stand up for his own human dignity and tell Gwede to piss off. Maybe the job meant much to him or maybe he could have been locked up summarily as well.

It was my turn. Gwede sat me on a chair in his office, opposite his. Between us was his large wooden desk. The desk was totally bare except for an old tape recorder and a horse-whip. Charles Ngwata sat on another chair but on Gwede's side.

"Yes, my friend! Why are you here?" Gwede asked me.

"You called for me," I replied.

He then pulled out the drawer of the desk and laid a sheath of blank paper on the desk. He pulled out another drawer, pulled out a revolver for me to see and then put it back. From his jacket he pulled out a BIC pen and got himself ready to write.

"Who appointed you to go into the Diplomatic Service?" he bellowed at me.

"You should know!" I said to him.

"I am asking you!" he retorted angrily.

"Listen," I said, "I never applied for the job. Nobody applies for that kind of job. I was just told that the President had appointed me to go into the Diplomatic Service. How the hell would I know who had recommended my name?"

Gwede tore up whatever he had been writing and tossed the pieces of paper into a waste-paper basket by his side.

"Alright, let us start again," he said getting another blank sheet of paper ready.

"Who did you meet while you were in the Diplomatic Service?" he asked.

I really thought it was an asinine question.

"You meet and see thousands of people everyday. And you ask me who I met in a period of over two years?" I replied.

"Okay, did you meet any of the rebels?" he asked me.

"Look," I said, "even if I met any of them now, I could not recognize them. I saw both Mr Kanyama Chiume and Mr Henry Chipembere, here on Malawi soil, when I was a young boy in secondary school and they were cabinet ministers."

"We know that. If you had met any of them we would have known immediately," replied Gwede boastfully.

"So, why did you ask me?" I said angrily as I stood up.

I leaned on his desk with my left hand and attempted to reach out for his shirt-collar with my right hand. Gun or no gun, I was going to punch his face. He drew back out of my reach.

"Alright, let us start again," he said when he realised that my temper was not as long as he thought it was. "Sit down. Do you want a cup of coffee?" he asked.

"I do not want your coffee!" I replied as I sat down.

He tore up the piece of paper he had been scribbling on and threw the bits into the waste-paper basket again.

"You came back from the Diplomatic Service over a year ago. Why were you still using a diplomatic passport? We found a diplomatic passport in your house!" he started again.

"Every time I go out of the country or come in, I pass through the Immigration. Are you suggesting that the Immigration Officers of Malawi do not recognize a Malawi diplomatic passport?" I asked him.

"Answer the question!" he demanded.

"For your information, I went to the Immigration Office immediately after my return from the Diplomatic Service. I gave them my diplomatic passport and asked for my ordinary passport, but they refused. They said that I should hang on to my diplomatic passport because they are wasting a lot of money. They exchange an ordinary passport for a diplomatic passport and a few months later the same person is appointed into the diplomatic service again. Ask them! Ring them now!" I said to him.

Gwede tore up the sheet he had been writing on and threw the pieces into the waste-paper basket.

"Alright, let us begin again," he said. "You wrote a book about the President. You said that he has no friends."

"Have you read the book?" I asked him.

"Answer me!" he demanded.

"*Nobody's Friend* is the title of the small novel I wrote. It has absolutely nothing to do with Dr Banda or anyone else. It is a book about ordinary people. It is fiction. You should have read it," I told him.

"But there is a passage about a president being assassinated in

38

that book," he said triumphantly.

"That is rubbish!" I said. "Have you read Hamlet, Macbeth or King Lear, all by William Shakespeare? There are passages in all those books about Kings being assassinated. Have you banned those books because they mention the assassination of Kings? Have you banned the Holy Bible because it mentions that Jesus was killed?"

"Let us begin again," Gwede said as he tore up the sheet of paper he had been writing on. He threw the pieces into the waste-paper basket. This time he did not bother to write again.

"Listen to me, my friend! You are finished, finished, finished! I am the last word on detention in Malawi. No one else is above me. As you sit there I have three options for you. Firstly, I can release you now. Yes, you can go home to your wife and back to your job. Secondly, I can take you to court for trial where you will get many years of imprisonment. Lastly, I can send you to Mikuyu Maximum Security Prison, without trial, where you will count the hair on your head. You will never come out. I have decided to send you to Mikuyu where others like you are rotting," he said chillingly. "As long as I sit on this chair, you will never come out. You will rot there!"

He said all this emphatically as he banged the top of the desk with his right-hand fist. I looked at him very defiantly.

"Gwede," I said, "last year, you were not sitting on that chair. Next year, you do not know if you will still be sitting on that chair. Only the Almighty God knows. If God has made it for me to live the rest of my life and die in Mikuyu prison, so be it. It is not you who has done it. You are just an instrument used by God. But I assure you that if God has not made it for me to die in Mikuyu, I shall come out alive and well. And much earlier than you think."

What I said unnerved him a bit. He had played his last card. He had failed to reduce me to a cowering, tearful coward, crying for mercy at his feet. The degree of my defiance shook his self-confidence thoroughly.

"You go for lunch. We shall meet again this afternoon," he said to me as he terminated the interrogation.

Charles Ngwata took me outside. Gwede closed the door of his office. A police constable brought me a plate of rice and red beans. What was strange was that they gave me a spoon as well. That was on Friday, 25 January 1975. My interrogation had taken Gwede's entire morning.

CHAPTER 5

Block B

I ate my lunch while expecting another stormy meeting with my tormentor, Gwede. He apparently had had enough of me. He did not want to see me again. Charles Ngwata took me back to Zomba Prison in the same unmarked police van. I went straight to my cell but he stayed on in the office of the Prison Superintendent.

Just before lock-up time, at four o'clock another day, I was called to the office. Two men from the Special Branch were there. I was asked if I was Sam Mpasu. I said yes, I was. Then they laid before me, on the table, Detention Order No. 1770 which they asked me to sign. In prison parlance that dreaded piece of paper was called a D.O. It was already signed by the President, Dr Hastings Kamuzu Banda, informing me that he was going to keep me in any prison anywhere in Malawi in the interests of preserving public security. It was a law under the National Security Public Order and Defence Act, a sweeping, draconian dragnet he had rammed through Parliament in 1965.

"Why should I countersign it?" I asked.

"Proof that you have read and understood it," they replied.

I countersigned it. Then they made me read a letter which was signed by the Principal Secretary of Trade and Industry informing me of my dismissal from the civil service. I was dismissed with immediate effect for security reasons and without terminal benefits. Although the letter was mine, they took it back. They never let me have it. In fact that was the first and last time I saw it.

The prison warder followed me back to my cell.

"Take out all your things. You are not staying here anymore," he said.

I was startled. He led me across the courtyard and across a fence of steel bars into the courtyard of another old two-storey block of cells. There were thousands of people there, a mixture of convicted prisoners, political detainees and mad men.

These people received me with a great deal of awe. Apparently, the first cell where I had been put was where the most dangerous prisoners went. In fact when, in 1972, a South African Airways plane had been hijacked by two Arabs and the hijack was foiled on Malawi soil one of those Arabs stayed in my cell. The impression these fellow prisoners had of me was that I was an extremely dangerous and armed opponent of the Malawi Government. I found that extremely comical.

When lock-up time came, a swarm of prison warders invaded our courtyard, armed with their wooden truncheons.

"Fall in!" their boss shouted.

At the mention of those words we all squatted on our haunches in lines of four, one behind the other. Then they counted us. After satisfying themselves that we were all in and none had escaped, they herded us into our cells.

The cell I was put in was the size of a small bedroom but there were twenty-two of us in there. Each cell had its own monitor, called a Nyapala. He had feudal powers over us. The powers of the prison officials were effectively delegated to him. He was in complete command in the cell as soon as the cell-door was closed behind us and locked.

The latest arrival slept next to the bucket. There were no beds, mattresses or mats. We all slept on the bare floor.

Our old blankets were literally crawling with thick, black lice which feasted on us throughout the night. The bucket was not big enough for twenty-two people, from four o'clock in the afternoon of one day to six o'clock in the morning of the following day. By about midnight that bucket was overflowing with human urine and excrement. It wetted our blankets and the floor. As if that was not dreadful enough, the whole prison was heavily infested with large, black rats. They ran all over us in the darkness, looking for a chance to nibble at our toes and heels. Fleas from the rats were even more troublesome to us than the lice.

Sleep was made impossible by two other events. One was the

wild, unintelligible singing of a schizophrenic, who apparently never slept. He was tall and filthy. During the day, he used to go to the garbage bin and eat from there. It was no use giving him food on a plate. He put the food on the ground and ate from there. Once I saw him chase a huge, black rat in broad daylight. He caught it just before it could squeeze itself into a hole. Squealing and squeaking, the rat was put into his mouth, head first, and it was chewed off. With its blood dripping from his lips, he finished off the raw rat, bit by bit, and squeezed its long tail into his mouth. It was a revolting sight, but he was not the only mad person around. There were at least a dozen of them. What characterized this man was his loud singing throughout the night. Living with the mad people was a daily scare. Perhaps it was part of the punishment.

The second event which deprived us of sleep was the singing of the people on death row. Our cell was next to the Condemned Cell Number One (CC1) where the gallows were. All the people who had been condemned to death by the courts and had exhausted their appeals were kept there. They were chained to steel hooks on the floor, all day, every day, waiting for execution. They were dressed in red T-shirts and were never let out of the cell until they were executed.

I was told that the executions were done four times a year, normally in February, April, August and November. A white man from South Africa was the official hangman but he used some of the prison warders for the dirty work. All he did was organise everything. I was told of a gruesome day when a total of fifty-eight people were executed in one night. The poor souls were stripped naked but had hoods over their heads before they were hanged. They were hanged three at a time. They were finished off with blows to the back of the skull, with a hammer or with powerful pliers which crushed their testicles. The naked corpses were then carried away by convicted prisoners who were serving sentences. They were tossed into a common grave and covered with earth.

Those condemned men who were not executed on a particular day lived in constant fear of being executed on the next occasion, three months away. They were singing solemn hymns every night and asking God for forgiveness. The most popular hymn was Number 347 in the Hymn Book of the Church of Central African Presbyterian (CCAP) which starts with: "Tate ndili mwana wanu nkana ndinachimwa" or "Father I am your child although I have sinned against you".

Those who were condemned to death, but had not yet exhausted their appeals, were also dressed in red T-shirts. They were kept in CC2. They too were never let out of the prison, although they were free to move about within the prison. They did not stay chained to the floor every day, all day.

Dr Banda was hanging hundreds of prisoners every year. Many of them had gone through the traditional courts system where the defence was not allowed legal representation but the prosecution was. It was very clear that many of those condemned men were totally innocent of the murder cases they were charged with. Their loud singing and prayers made this very clear. The traditional courts system made it very easy for Malawians to frame each other and to have an enemy judicially murdered.

A shocking, terrible story was told of a man in Karonga who had fallen victim to a carefully thought out plan. He was rescued a few days before he was executed. A certain man from Tanzania who had lived for many years in Karonga, and had worked as a tailor, was told by a local chief to go back to Tanzania immediately and never come back. He did. His sudden disappearance was then attributed to a murder. The murder was attributed to an enemy of the chief. The accused man was confronted in the traditional court by an array of false witnesses. They were in the pay of the local chief. He lost the case and lost the appeal. He consequently earned himself a death sentence. No attempt was made to substantiate the allegation of murder by producing the body or any shred of evidence.

"You killed the person, you produce the body," he was told, quite logically.

One day, a close relative of the condemned man crossed the Songwe River into Tanzania on some other unrelated business.

By some strange coincidence, he saw the tailor in a market. There was no time for niceties. He dashed back into Malawi to collect a group of other relatives. The tailor was forcibly abducted into Malawi and told to cooperate. By producing the person who was supposed to have been murdered, the villagers saved their own relative from the gallows just in the nick of time. He had been due to be hanged for the murder of a person who was still alive and well in Tanzania.

Everytime the condemned prisoners learned that Dr Banda, the Life-President, had come to Zomba from Blantyre, they knew that he had come to sign the execution warrants. Whether it was superstition or not, Dr Banda never stayed in Zomba on the night of the executions. When the police siren of his long motorcade wailed, as it sped by the prison fence on his way to Blantyre, the men on death row feared the worst.

Many of them knew on a Thursday that their time was up. On that Thursday those whose names were not on the execution warrants were unchained and taken away to another cell. Those who remained chained on their floor hooks were the ones to be executed that weekend.

On Friday morning, they were unchained and allowed to say good-bye to their relatives. The relatives would have been summoned to the prison before-hand. Some of the relatives could not stand the strain. They went away sobbing as the condemned men gave instructions regarding who was going to inherit which chicken, which goat or which pair of trousers.

Zomba prison was like the Reuters News Agency as far as information on the outside world was concerned. It was a well-informed place through clandestine news gatherers. Long-serving and trusted convicted prisoners were allowed to go and work outside. They were the type of prisoners who would be sent to the shop all alone and never think of escaping. They were loyal to a fault; completely trusted. They were sent to do chores in hospital wards, army or police offices and even at State House itself. When they went to State House to cut grass they were very observant. If they saw medical doctors at State House, we knew that Dr

Banda had fallen very sick, well beyond the competence of his personal physicians. Quite often, that kind of news was cause for celebration, in eager anticipation of his early demise. That was how much he was hated by the people in the prison. If they saw a Cabinet Minister summoned to State House but drive away without the pennant flying on the bonnet of his official car, we knew that the minister had been summarily dismissed. Quite often our news analysis was correct.

Sometimes the convicted prisoners were taken to clean up offices at the Police Headquarters or Army Barracks. While there, they took every opportunity to glance quickly at confidential documents to tell us. You see, once a person is in that prison uniform, it is difficult for anyone to differentiate between the one who went to school and the other who did not.

Other prisoners were simply interested in sex. Whenever they were taken to work in the houses of the army, police or prison officers, they were quick to seduce the officers' wives. They came back to compare notes. It was considered quite an achievement when, one day, one of them told the others that he had made love to a woman police officer in uniform, on the carpet, in her own office.

Sometimes it was difficult to know who was doing the seduction in view of the kind of gifts the prisoners brought back into prison. It was absolutely unbelievable how they were smuggling in goodies such as cigarettes, bottles of vaseline jelly, loaves of bread or even Coca-Cola bottles. They were really ingenious. Some of the small items were squeezed into the anus. The man walked through the rigorous checks easily. Some of the big items were brought in with the assistance of the prison warders, without their knowledge. For example, a prisoner would subserviently offer to carry the prison warder's heavy coat and then tuck in the items. It was a very serious offence for any of those items to be found in prison but they were there in large quantities every day. Regular weekly inspections were done. Almost invariably, sackfuls of smuggled things were taken away. The food items and drinks were eaten by the prisoners, at night, after lockup. They were rare and valuable luxuries. Even money was plenty in that prison. Bank notes exchanged hands easily and yet Zomba Central Prison is perhaps one of the toughest in the country.

CHAPTER 6

The Stories of Block B

It was not just some of the people on death row who were innocent but still suffered. The defective Traditional Courts system gave some people plenty of latitude for abuses. They got others officially killed or locked away for a very long time. The law on the preservation of public order, defence and national security, which underpinned imprisonment-without-trial, also gave some people, especially policemen, plenty of latitude for other forms of abuses. This law was a sieve through which anyone could get rid of a tiresome neighbour. It was also possible for anyone to get rid of a person who had a beautiful and desirable wife if she was resisting amorous advances.

Using the law to victimize fellow Malawians became a favourite pastime for many unscrupulous Malawians. Most of the political prisoners Dr Banda ranted about were far from political and still far less his enemies. But he was on adrenaline. He did not know or care that his own minions were using him for personal and private vendettas.

There was this young psychiatrist who had been running the Zomba Mental Hospital. He was with us in Block B as a temporary detainee. The word temporary did not mean anything. Many of them had been there for two years or longer. This doctor was born and brought up on the Copperbelt in Zambia. His Malawian parents had been working there. He had done all his schooling in Zambia and subsequently had gone to Britain for his medical training on a Zambian scholarship. After qualifying, he did not feel like working in Zambia. He never considered himself a Zambian. Instead, he came to Malawi bubbling with idealism and patriotism, anxious to help in developing his own motherland. He was the only psychiatrist in the country at the time. He ended up being in charge of the country's only Mental Hospital in Zomba.

His long stay in Zambia furnished plenty of ammunition for those who wanted to get rid of him. A whisper was made to the Special Branch. All they said was that this doctor was in fact an agent of the political exiles who had fled from Malawi and were living in Zambia. The men of the Special Branch had a credo to act first and investigate later, if ever. The doctor was whisked off straight into Zomba Prison from his office at the mental hospital. I found him there. He had already done a few months by the time I came in. Since there was no psychiatrist to look after the patients in the mental hospital, all the mental patients were locked up with us, together with their doctor, in Zomba Prison.

Then, quite often, we would receive a batch of young men from Zimbabwe, then called Rhodesia. They were really primary school or secondary school age. They fled from schools in that country intending to go for guerilla training abroad. They were determined to do something for their own country. They wanted to fight Ian Smith who had unilaterally declared independence for Rhodesia. These young men had walked on foot, through the bushes, through Mozambique into Malawi. There, they expected understanding and sympathy. Instead, they were locked up with us in Zomba Prison. Whether they were handed over to Ian Smith or allowed to proceed to Tanzania for their military training, I have no idea. But they spent several weeks at a time and then disappeared suddenly. They were always collected at night and without notice. Whatever happened to them afterwards, these young men were bitter over their unexpected incarceration. Mozambican guerilla fighters were also regularly thrown into Zomba Prison. They, too, disappeared suddenly in the middle of the night, after a week or so.

Then there was this cheerful man. He had a genital organ which was longer than average. He was in prison because of it. He had done more than three months when I joined him there. Apparently he had a girlfriend towards whom he had noble intentions. He had never made love to her until the night of their wedding. That was a terrible and costly mistake. The young bride

49

experienced excruciating pain. She inwardly blamed him for not being gentle enough with her. She kept her anger to herself and was definitely not in the mood for a second round.

When the eager husband attempted to have her again, that night, she walked out from the bedroom into the night, without a word to him. He thought that she had gone to the toilet but she had gone straight to the chairman of the Malawi Congress Party branch. Love had suddenly turned into bitter hatred because of the pain. She had made up her mind to get rid of the cruel husband who had given her so much pain.

She told the chairman a lie that her new husband had already started beating her up. For evidence, she produced a broken string of waist beads which, she said, had broken during the struggle. Immediately, that same night the chairman sent his unofficial policemen, the members of the Youth League, to fetch the husband. The young man had absolutely no idea about what was afoot. He was still lying naked on his bed, eagerly waiting for the return of his young bride from the toilet, when the political thugs broke in. They jumped on him and pummelled him to their hearts' content. Then they dragged him, half-dressed, before the chairman. His arms were tied at the back. The chairman wrote a note to the police to the effect that the man had ill-treated one of Dr Banda's women or *mbumba*. On the strength of that note, the police locked him up in Zomba Prison, without a word or charge. We all sympathised with the cheerful young man whose marriage had fallen victim to Dr Banda's brand of politics.

Then there was this Welshman friend of mine by the name of Harry Edwards. I had known him years before when we founded the first Chapter of Junior Chamber International (Jaycees) in Blantyre. He was married to a Malawian lady and was doing sawmilling as a business. He had suddenly disappeared from circulation. I had no idea that he had been locked up. Here he was in Block B with me. He had already done several years in prison. At this time he was trying to regain his British citizenship as the only way he could escape from imprisonment without trial. The law applied to Malawi citizens only. Foreigners could only be deported because they owed no allegiance to Malawi.

A fishmonger provided another sad story. This man had gone to Lake Malawi to buy fish for resale in his home village. On the way from the lake he developed a problem in his bowels. He leaned the heavily laden bicycle on a roadside tree. He then walked into the bush to squat behind a shrub. After he had attended to the call of nature, he walked back to his bicycle on the roadside. There he found a police landrover waiting for him. He was accused of having fled into the bush after he had seen the police vehicle approaching. To the policemen, this was a clear sign that he had committed an offence. All his protests about bowels were ignored. The police refused to go and see the evidence behind the shrub. He was tossed into the back of the landrover, together with his bicycle and basket of fish, straight to Zomba prison. The fish rotted and were discarded. The man and his bicycle were still in prison.

"We shall release you when you tell us the crime you committed", the Special Branch people told him confidently.

A man who had been cuckolded by an office colleague told us another sad case. He was working in Salima. He was totally unaware that his wife was having an affair with his own colleague in the office. Their arrangement was simple. As soon as he came into the office in the morning, the workmate pretended to have forgotten a pen at his home. With that plausible excuse, the workmate walked out of the office but straight to the man's bedroom. On this fateful day, everything went on as usual, except that the cuckold had also forgotten his own pen at home. The two were already in the bedroom, making arrangements, when the wife saw her husband through the parted window curtains, walking back to the house. She feared for the worst and fled. The philanderer went round the house and returned to the office as if nothing had happened. The husband, who had seen nothing and suspected nothing, picked up his pen and returned to the office. The wife, in her desperate panic, ran to the chairman of the Malawi Congress Party branch. She showed him a Malawi Congress Party membership card which she had torn up.

"Look at this," she said, "my husband says he is fed up with all the MCP meetings I attend."

As far as the Malawi Congress Party chairman was concerned, the act of tearing up the MCP membership card was an act of treason. He sent the dreaded Youth League members to collect the man from the office. They roughed him up before they took him to the chairman. The chairman delivered him into police hands as soon as possible. The police in Salima could not handle such a hot potato. They sent him straight to the Regional Police Headquarters in Lilongwe. They too could not handle such a hot potato. They sent him straight to Zomba Police Headquarters who sent him straight into Zomba Prison.

The man had absolutely no idea about the allegation that he had torn up his own wife's MCP membership card. He had not even known that his own wife was behind it until she visited him six months later to confess it all. She boldly told the police to lock her up in prison and release her innocent husband. The police were at a loss with this strange turn of events. The man had already spent six months in jail and had lost his job.

Another day, a Swiss young man found himself one of us, in prison. He was a tourist, hitch-hiking his way from South Africa, back to Switzerland. As he walked along the streets of Zomba, some members of the Women's League of the Malawi Congress Party objected to his bell-bottom pair of trousers. The police had no option but to lock him up. One of their procedures before locking up a person was to search him. As they physically searched this young man, they found a big roll of marijuana around the waist band of his pair of trousers. He called it "grass" and had just bought it in a back street of Zomba for his own use and sale in Europe. He was very fortunate because the police decided to treat his problem as a criminal rather than a political offence. He was charged with the offences of wearing a bell-bottom pair of trousers and being in possession of forbidden drugs. He paid the fine and left.

An airline clerk paid very dearly for his marital infidelity. He had been working for Zambia Airways in Blantyre. He was happily married. As soon as they were blessed with a baby the wife insisted on going home up in the north, to show the baby to her parents. She had gone barely a week when the man started an affair with a single lady. Unknown to him the single lady had marital intentions.

The trouble started when the wife wrote the husband a letter about her return. The husband showed the letter to the girlfriend and requested her that their affair should come to an end. The girlfriend was not the type which takes heart-break news easily. She went to Albert Muwalo, the powerful Administrative Secretary and Secretary-General of the Malawi Congress Party at that time. There, she brewed up an imaginary story to the effect that she was being forced to undergo a dangerous back-street abortion by the man who had made her pregnant. That was enough. No effort was made to prove if she was really pregnant. Before she reached her home in Ndirande New Lines, the man was already in police hands and on his way to Zomba Prison.

The wife was very surprised when she was not met by her husband at the bus station. She went to the house but found it empty. She went to the office and found that it was empty too. That is where she learnt about her husband's imprisonment without trial. As a result of that imprisonment, he lost both his job and house. The wife became destitute. She had to go back to the village for family support.

A forgery expert had his spell too. His name was Nakhumwa. This Malawian had come home to Mulanje, on holiday, from Zambia where he worked. His work was very strange; he was a rich thief. Anyway, before his holiday was over, he found himself an inmate of Zomba Prison. His very expensive BMW car had its seats cut up and its tyres slashed by the Special Branch who were ostensibly looking for hidden weapons. Actually this man, by his own account, lived on company payrolls in Zambia.

He targeted companies which had large payrolls. He learned as much as possible about them regarding their pay day, the uniform of their security men, the size and make of their huge metal-box for cash and so forth. Then he befriended the messenger of that company to bring him a used bank cheque. Once he got such a used bank cheque he spent many days practising the signatures of that company's cheque signatories. When the pay day approached, he mounted a similar operation to the one which was usually mounted by the company. But his would be at the bank thirty minutes earlier. He was very daring really. That way he went away with an entire company's monthly pay-roll, in cash. Quite often, it was just a few minutes before the company itself tried to get the cash. He hit Lusaka and lay low for a couple of months. Then he hit Livingstone and lay low for some time. Later he would hit a town on the Copperbelt and lie low. He circulated like that and the Zambian Police never got him.

When he came to his home village in Mulanje, he met a cousin of his. Unknown to him, she was a girlfriend of a senior man in the Special Branch. In a fit of jealousy over the money he showered around, the Special Branch officer framed him, as a political agent of Malawi exiles. That is how he found himself in Zomba Prison.

He had a reputation for magic even in the prison. Whenever the warders surrounded and clobbered him, they went off on sick leave. It was they who suffered from the beating. Whenever they dragged him into the punishment cell, they could not chain him to the floor. The lock never worked and the chain fell down. In the end they had to leave him alone by appealing to his sense of honour. They were happy if he just went through the motions of the punishment.

Chief Ngamwano from Thyolo was completely bewildered. He had been thrown into Zomba Prison without charge or trial. All he knew was that he had lent some money to a local functionary of the Malawi Congress Party in his area in Thyolo. He had never said anything against Dr Banda or his government and had certainly never tried to recover the loan from the MCP functionary.

That month, January 1975, Chief Ngamwano received letters from his headquarters. Among the letters was a Christmas card to him from Dr Banda. It was news all over the prison. It was proof, if proof was needed, that Dr Banda did not even know that a powerful traditional chief from Thyolo had been locked up in his name. Chief Ngamwano was not an ordinary run-of-the-mill chief. He had played a prominent role in the political struggle against the white settlers and federal administrations. News went round that he had personally used magic to get a swarm of killer bees to sting and chase away the troops which had come to quell disturbances in Thyolo in 1959.

Knowing Dr Banda's irrational temper, it was indeed strange that he had not deposed Chief Ngamwano. The truth of the matter was that the Malawi Congress Party functionary did not want to repay the loan to the chief. The only way to kill the debt was to have the chief locked away, on the basis of some lies to the Special Branch. Chief Ngamwano never made it home. He fell sick and died in Zomba Prison. They did not bother to take him to the hospital. On his last day, they locked him up in a punishment cell where he struggled with death the whole day. He screamed and kicked about against the walls. They opened the door only when he fell silent and was dead. The body was taken out and sent home.

A day in Block B of Zomba Prison was never dull. One advantage we had was the availability of plenty of water. We could take a shower at any time during the day. Of course without soap or a towel, because we were temporary detainees. We had our comical events as well. For example, we had to compete for concrete space in the courtyard when the sun was really hot. We wanted to spread our lice-infested blankets in the sun in order to drive them away from the blanket. The theory was that the less the lice in the blanket, the less would be the bites in the night.

While we spread the blankets in the hot sun, we ourselves would be competing for a spot of shade for cover. It was dreadful but it was like that, day in, day out. Just sitting and doing nothing, no radio to listen to, no newspaper to read, no book to read and no game to play. What was even more frustrating was the total uncertainty about release day. The convicted prisoners were better off; they knew the exact day of the end of their sentences. We did not know ours. We were suspended in a limbo of uncertainty.

The ground floor of Block B housed the punishment cells, popularly known as Ku Mdima, or place of darkness. One day, a group of prison warders responded to a whistle-call near the prison kitchen. There, they clubbed down a convicted prisoner who had started a fisticuff fight with a Nyapala. In no time at all they carried him half-conscious, by holding his arms and legs like a four-cornered blanket, into one of the punishment cells in our block. They chained him to the floor. Then they poured four pailfuls of cold water over him. The water did not flow out because the floor was made to hold it in. It formed a pool in the cell. He stayed chained in that pool like that for two days without food to eat or water to drink. In his position he was completely helpless. He could not urinate or defecate decently. On the third day, he was a completely subdued man. Weak, hungry and with his limbs numb, he was suing for mercy to no avail. They kept him there for another three days.

We nearly had a tragedy one day. A young boy in his early teens was imprisoned. They threw him in on remand to await trial for whatever crime he had committed. The homosexuals were very excited over him. They eyed him with lust all day. An argument soon broke out on the question of who was going to sleep next to him. The principle of the latest comer sleeping next to the bucket was obviously not going to apply to that boy. The Nyapala moved very fast to put down the rebellion over the unsuspecting boy. He went to the prison office where he spun out a story against the main challenger. It was totally untrue but the place had its own moral values and standards. The challenger suddenly found himself being clubbed down with truncheons by the prison warders. As he lay on the ground groaning in pain, and professing his innocence, he was dragged by the legs and arms into the punishment cell in our Block B.

They locked him up in the punishment cell but did not take away his clothes. They did not chain him to the floor either. The thought of losing that delicate boy to another man was intolerable to the challenger; it was worse than death.

As soon as the door was locked, he started to work. He used his fingernails to cut the prison uniform into strips. With these strips he made a good noose around his neck. Holding the loose end of the rope in one hand, he made several attempts to jump up to the top end of the cell door. There were tough thick steel bars on top of the door. He succeeded to get hold of one and tied the loose end of the rope to it. He presently let go of himself. His bodyweight instantly tugged at the noose to make it tighter and tighter. As his life ebbed away, his body started to swing from side to side like a pendulum. This was when we noticed it. We saw the near lifeless face through the steel bars up above the wooden door. And we heard the legs banging aimlessly against the door. He was dying but there was nothing we could do to save him because the door was locked. We could not get at him. We started shouting for attention. The prison warders came running. They unlocked the padlock, pulled back the bolt and opened the door. Then they hurriedly cut the rope. He fell to the floor, almost dead.

He was rushed to the clinic where they managed to save his life. They did not leave him loose this time. His hands and feet were chained to prevent him from attempting another suicide. It seemed that he genuinely felt like dying rather than see that boy in the hands of another man. Some people do not value their own lives at all. I totally failed to understand the actions of this man. Giving up his life because of thwarted sexual gratification was something I could not understand. But then I have heard of some men dying for women and some women dying for men. This was the first time I saw a man trying to die because of another man.

After he had recovered sufficiently in the clinic, he was brought back to the punishment cell, the prison within the prison, to finish his sentence. This time they gave him a severe beating, stripped him of all the clothing and chained him to the floor. Then they poured several pails of cold water over him. He stayed like that for days, rolling in water, day and night and totally naked, like an animal. The first two days he was not given any food or water. On the third day, he was more than grateful for the half ration he received. Apparently he was now anxious to preserve his life.

CHAPTER 7

Trip to Mikuyu

I have no doubt in my mind that, had the police kept me in Zomba Prison for only one day, I was going to live in perpetual fear of Dr Hastings Kamuzu Banda and his prisons, for the rest of my life. The long stay inured me. I became used to the rhythms of life in that lower world. I had been in a state of shock for a long time, but it began to wear off rather fast. I promised myself that if ever I would get a chance to contribute, however little, towards the removal of Dr Banda's evil and cruel system, I would do so with all my heart.

My stay in Zomba Prison had an unexpected side effect. It brought me closer to God. From 1969 until 1975, when I was thrown into prison, I had never stepped into a church for prayers. The only exception was in Cologne in Germany, in 1972, when my Nigerian secretary was getting married. I had given up on the church altogether but I had not entirely given up on God. I had remained a believer in God. I prayed in the privacy of my home before sleep at night, after sleep in the morning and at meals. But I stayed away from church.

The incident which had taken me out of the church was a sermon at the St. Michaels and All Angels Church in Blantyre, popularly called H.H.I. When I lived in Ndirande New Lines, I regularly went to that church for prayers. This Sunday, in November 1969, I was stunned by the sermon.

The black preacher, who preached in English that day, devoted the whole sermon to Dr Hastings Kamuzu Banda. He referred to him as a messiah and a saviour who had been sent by God to save the people of Malawi. Jesus Christ hardly got a mention in that sermon.

Elevating a fellow human being to the level of divinity was

something I was totally incapable of appreciating. To me, the church had been prostituted for crass political ends. It could not give me the spiritual strength I needed anymore. I never told anyone, but that day I stopped going to church, any church. If the people who had taken serious religious vows to look after our spiritual health were the first in line to sink that low, what hope had I? Let them keep their church, I said. What shocked me most was the fact that this was in the midst of the Chilobwe political murders when newly married couples were getting brutally axed to death in their own bedrooms at night and their genitals removed.

The first thing that struck me in Zomba Prison was that there was a genuine church inside its walls. There were no preachers, no bibles, no korans, and no hymn books in Zomba Prison; they were not allowed. But the love of God and the quest for salvation was burning in the hearts of the prisoners. Most touching were those on the death row. I dreaded to think that many of them were about to be executed for crimes they had never committed. They knew it and said so to God. They wondered aloud why God was permitting all the injustices and evil schemes in the world to succeed. What was very touching was their submission to God's will. They had given up on this world; they did not care about it anymore. What they cared about was their lives in the hereafter.

I began to think seriously about myself in a philosophical manner. I looked at my fellow prisoners, both convicted and political. We were an assortment of rich people and poor people, businessmen and employees, traditional chiefs and clergymen, civil servants and soldiers. Dr Banda's harsh laws had swept us all into that hell. We were cut off from our loved ones and from everything we owned. We were the living dead. Many of us had no idea whatsoever why we were going through that hell on earth. We were utterly helpless.

A cattle-rustler used to rub the salt in. He had a nasty way of joking about our fate. This man had the courage to raid Dr Banda's ranch and get away with several head of cattle. By the time they got him, he had sold all of them. But they recovered those which had not yet been slaughtered. Expectedly, he was serving a very long sentence. Because of his long sentence he had graduated, through seniority, into a Nyapala.

As Nyapala he had vast powers over us, political prisoners. He knew it and we knew it. He boasted quite regularly about it.

"Within the walls of this prison," he used to say, "you are all in my hands. When I say: Fall-in, you all fall-in immediately, because you know what I can do to you. But I know that outside this prison, I am not fit to be your domestic servant, not even a gardener or a messenger in your big offices.

"Look at them," he said, pointing at the prison warders, "they do not have the high education you have. They do not earn the kind of money you earn. They do not enjoy the status in society which you enjoy. They cannot even get close to those beautiful wives of yours who come to visit you in your expensive cars. Many of them cannot afford a bicycle. But here, here in this prison, they can clobber you at will, any time. They can hang you if they are told to."

What he said was entirely true. It was quite sobering. It was a measure of the extent to which we had been destroyed.

One day I was called to the office. I was pleasantly surprised to see my wife there. She had come to visit me. We stood on opposite sides of a wire mesh. A man from the Special Branch stood nearby to listen to every word we spoke to each other. All we had were fifteen minutes.

She told me of how most of my friends and her friends were trying their best to run away from her. They did not want to be seen near the wife of a political prisoner. They did not want to be accused of sympathizing with Dr Banda's enemies. Their own jobs, and indeed personal freedoms, depended on it. She told me how she had moved out of the government house we had been living in. Then she told me of how the Malawi Police had seized my private car, under the suspicion that I had probably used a government car-loan to purchase it.

Their senseless act really enraged me. How mean and petty were they going to be? I had used a bank loan to purchase that car

60

when I was in Germany. My own employers, the Malawi Government, had refused to grant me a car-loan on the grounds that another car I had left unsold in Malawi had also used a government car-loan. I had spent two months hitching a ride from my German landlords. What kind of diplomat does that? And here the Malawi police were, taking that car away from my pregnant wife, just at the time when she badly needed a car. I felt like exploding with anger. The thought of their having forced my pregnant wife into an overcrowded bus, all the way from Blantyre to Zomba and back, really made me furious.

I asked for a piece of paper and a pencil. I wrote a terse, short note to the Officer-in-Charge of Blantyre Police Station. I told him to release the car to my wife immediately. I did not specify what action I was going to take if he did not do what I said. I gave the note to my wife.

"Give this note to him today as soon as you arrive in Blantyre," I said to her.

He must have been very surprised with the tone of my note. He was sufficiently intimidated, however, for he released the car to her immediately.

I had been in Zomba Prison since the 22 January 1975. During the night of Valentines Day, 14 February 1975, the door of my cell was opened by three warders, as usual wielding their thick truncheons. They called out my name. Many of my cell mates were fast asleep. Those who heard me called out minded their own business.

"Pick up all your things and come out," they said in low voices.

Picking up things in a cell which was pitch dark, in the middle of the night, was not easy. I staggered outside. They bolted and locked the cell door. They led me to the office block. As soon as we entered the office, one of them pulled out a pair of handcuffs. He clamped them on me. The small bundle of items of clothing, which had constituted all my personal possessions in that prison, were thrown on the festoon of my handcuffed hands. He picked up a gun at the corner, checked that it was loaded and pointed at the door.

"Let us go!" he said.

"Where are we going?" I asked.

"Don't ask. Come on!" he pushed me towards the door.

Outside the outer prison door a landrover was waiting for me. The driver was on the steering wheel. The engine was on. The armed guard opened the door of the cab and ordered me in. He came in after me. There were just the three of us. I was between the driver and the armed guard. My hands were in handcuffs. There was no one else at the back of the car.

The car moved out of the prison fence to join the main road. It turned left towards Lilongwe. The streets of Zomba were deathly quiet as the car sped along. We did not speak to each other in the car. The driver's job was to drive and not ask questions. The guard's job was to take me wherever he was told to.

I was filled with fear. I trembled at the thought that I was going to be murdered in cold blood in the middle of the night. I trembled at the thought that my body was going to be disposed of in a manner which would not allow me to have a proper burial by my loved ones. I closed my eyes. I said a prayer in my heart. I asked the Almighty God to forgive and receive me in His arms.

Having been taken out of the cell in the middle of the night, I was certain that none of my cell-mates would ever know where I had been taken to. There were lots of people who had simply disappeared in the night. Sometimes large groups of people. We saw them in the afternoon, but they were no longer there with us in the morning. We did not know where they had been taken to or what had happened to them. We did not even dare to ask. Now the same thing was happening to me. No one else in the world would ever be able to tell my family what was going to befall me that day.

I confess that I was in the grip of terrible fear. I was tortured by the thought that we were heading for Liwonde on the road to Lilongwe. I had heard terrifying stories, on the grapevine, that the Kamuzu Barrage, across the Shire River at Liwonde, was their favourite place for killing political opponents. Stories were told of some people who had been trussed up and then put in sacks together with large rocks. The sacks were then properly tied at the top. The poor fellows would be kept like that the whole day, hardly able to breathe. During the night, the loaded sacks were taken to the Kamuzu Barrage on the backs of Malawi Congress Party landrovers or Malawi Young Pioneer landrovers and then tossed into the water.

I had never really believed those stories because I thought they were too barbaric to be true. A colleague I was with in the Diplomatic Service confirmed them. His own father, who was a minor politician in Zomba, had miraculously survived such a gruesome experience. The man had been summoned for urgent business to the Malawi Congress Party district office in Zomba, very early in the morning. On arrival, he was told to enter a certain room and wait for the bosses. He was then immediately surrounded by the Youth League thugs. He was beaten up thoroughly with wooden sticks. No questions were asked or answers sought. They just beat him. No one came to his rescue, or responded to his cries for mercy. His elbows and knee caps were knocked out into numbness before he was tied up and bagged. The sack was taken into a waiting landrover and driven to a secure house at a place called LETTER BOX. He spent the whole day in that sack trying to ease up the tight ropes. He heard voices of ordinary people as they passed by, but he could not shout for help because his mouth had been properly gagged.

During the evening the Youth League thugs came for him. He was tossed over into the water at Kamuzu Barrage in Liwonde. What helped him was the fact that they did not check if the ropes were still tight. His complete quietness also made them believe that he had already died. Through last-minute, frantic efforts as the sack hit the water surface, the rope came off at the mouth. He slipped out as the sack went down, weighted by the rock. Although his legs were still tied up, his hands had been loosened. He was able to swim away towards the reeds on the river bank. He just had time to see the red tail-lights of the landrover as it drove away.

He grabbed a reed and paused to recover his breath. His fear was now over crocodiles. He made as little noise as possible as he pulled himself over the bank. Once on the bank, in that sodden state, he untied his legs and started to walk home. He walked along the same road back to his village near Domasi, ducking into the roadside bush whenever he saw vehicle headlights approaching. He told the story to his wife before he fell asleep due to extreme exhaustion.

In the morning of that day, a prominent local politician went to that village to call for elections. He told the unsuspecting villagers that their chairman, meaning the man they had attempted to drown, had turned into a traitor and had fled to Zambia to join other exiles for war against Dr Banda. The villagers were reluctant to believe the story. The prominent politician chided them for not believing his word. He challenged them to go and check at the man's house. It was at this moment when the victim emerged from the house to respond to the enquiries of his fellow villagers. As soon as his eyes met those of the prominent politician, an indescribable event took place. The prominent politician thought that he was face-to-face with a ghost. He was thoroughly shaken as he hurriedly dashed for his Mercedes Benz car. He drove away in humiliation and shame.

I remembered this story as the car sped away into the night. I wondered if this meant that I was the next candidate for crocodile dinner. What puzzled me was that the men, as prison warders, were civil servants. They were not members of the Malawi Young Pioneer Movement or the Youth League of Malawi. Another cause for surprise was that I was merely handcuffed. I was not bagged. I wondered if they were going to shoot me dead in the night before they tossed my body into the river. Or if they were going to drown me with my hands handcuffed.

Very soon the car left the lit streets of Zomba behind. The lights of the car cut a swathe through the darkness. The tension in me was rising as I realised that the distance to Liwonde would take no more than thirty minutes. Those could be the last thirty minutes of my life.

Totally unexpectedly, the car turned right. It left the main road.

That perplexed me more. We drove past the Zomba Military Airport and continued on the road to Jali. I had no idea now where we were going. It was very dark outside except for the section of the road where the headlights lit. Suddenly a road sign came into view. It said simply: MIKUYU PRISON FARM. The car turned left into that road. I was so relieved to realise that I was being sent to Mikuyu Maximum Security Prison as Focus Gwede had promised me. I was not being taken to a place of instant murder as I had feared.

A short distance later, a high wire fence came into view on our right. Staff houses were on the left and the road was between. The car continued and then turned right to stop in front of the gate. After formalities, the car was allowed to drive through. It stopped right in front of the office block inside the wire fence. The whole place was well lit up with spot lights right round the wire fence.

The armed guard got out of the car and ordered me out. He led me to the large wooden door where he knocked. Someone from inside looked at us through a peep-hole before he opened the door. I was led to sit down on the floor of the corridor. After an exchange of words, a piece of paper was handed over. The armed guard who brought me walked back to his car, only to come back hurriedly. He had forgotten his handcuffs. He leaned down with a key in his hand. He inserted the key and removed the irons from me. I was immensely relieved to have them taken away. They were the type that gets tighter with the slightest movement. They were crushing the bones in my wrist.

CHAPTER 8

Mikuyu Prison

There are two separate prisons at Mikuyu. One is for convicted prisoners whose hard-labour sentences consist mostly of working on the prison farm. The farm itself is over two hundred-acres large. It is used for growing maize for feeding the prison population in and around Zomba. It is situated almost half a kilometre away from the other Mikuyu Prison.

Closer to the road is the infamous Mikuyu Maximum Security Prison for political prisoners. It is enclosed in a high-wire security fence which is brightly lit all round at night. Inside that fence is a rectangular building whose walls are built of burnt-clay bricks. The building is divided into large rooms which serve as cells. In front of each cell is a yard which is also marked by a high brick fence. The entire top of the yard is covered with reinforced steel wire-mesh to prevent the inmates from flying out, if ever they developed wings. In front of these yards is an open courtyard. At one end of this rectangular structure is the office of the Officer-In-Charge. It has an upper floor where his office was situated. From there he could see what was going on in all the yards of the cells. The visitors' room as well as the siren were also up there. On the ground floor was the store for the civilian clothing which they took away from us. It was on the left side of the ground floor, with a series of punishment cells on the right.

Directly opposite the office block is Cell A and the shower room. Cell A has a series of small rooms almost as long as a coffin and just as wide. It was for those on solitary confinement. Cell A reminded me of dog kennels. When I arrived at Mikuyu, Cell A had people such as the late Arthur Chipembere, Machipisa Munthali, Dr. Dennis Nkhwazi, Chakufwa Chihana and the late Augustine Munthali as its inmates. They were considered to be

66

the most dangerous political prisoners.

Cell B was immediately to the right after the office-block. Its inmates were mostly those of us who had travelled outside the country or whose allegations involved people out of the country.

Immediately after Cell B was Cell C. There was Cell C1 and C2. Those in C were considered to be normal political critics or opponents of Dr. Banda's rule. Both Cells B and C were directly opposite Cell D where there was D1, D2 and D3. The kitchen was there. Cell D was considered to be for those Malawians whose allegations were based purely on Malawi politics and, for some reason or other, less dangerous political prisoners. The former Cabinet Minister and Speaker of the National Assembly, the late Alec Nyasulu, was in Cell D.

Every square inch of the ground is covered in concrete. We never saw a blade of green grass, let alone a shrub or a tree. Once inside the Mikuyu Maximum Security Prison, your fate was sealed. There was only one day in the year on which you could be considered for release. That day was Kamuzu Day, 14 May. Once the day came and passed, you had to brace yourself for another twelve months and hope the Kamuzu Day of the following year would be your lucky day. The only way you could come out of Mikuyu Prison, on a day other than Kamuzu Day, was through death. There were many deaths occurring at that time. Both the poor quality of the food and the harsh living conditions were designed to accelerate the death of the inmates.

The most dangerous thing you could ever do at Mikuyu Prison was to fall sick. Your death was almost certain thereafter. There was a rudimentary clinic which was in one of the punishment cells. It was run by one man who had retired from the army. His limited knowledge of diseases and drugs clearly showed that even in the army he had been no higher than a clinic cleaner. He spent nearly all his time drinking Kachasu. He was always drunk.

He usually opened the door of the cell yard abruptly and called for only five sick people. The first five would sprint through the door. Then he shut it. This system meant that those who were very sick were not able to make it to the door. They got no treatment.

There was no question of making him change his mind about the number of sick people he had arbitrarily imposed. When anyone became very sick, they came to take him away from us. They put him, all alone, in a punishment cell. This too meant that the sick man would never have the assistance of his cell-mates for a drink of water or to fan him with a shirt when he became short of breath. Quite often, the sick people who were taken to the punishment cell, as the hospital ward, never came back. They died there. We knew that one had died when they came to collect away his blanket from our cell. Within an hour or two a landrover would be heard driving in and then driving out. They took the dead man's body to Zomba Prison.

Whenever a death occurred we were stunned. It was very clear to all of us that it was a question of "there, but for the grace of God, go I".

CHAPTER 9

Cell B

I was made to sit on the floor of the corridor until daybreak. At six o'clock in the morning there was a change of guards. The new shift came. Together with the old shift, they went from cell to cell to count the prisoners physically. This check was to ensure that none had escaped during the night.

After the counting, they came for me. I was told to strip naked completely. They gave me the prison uniform and ordered me to put it on. I put my legs through the pair of shorts and pulled it up. The waist was small. The pair of shorts came up to my upper thighs.

"You are too fat," said the prison warder angrily as he searched for a razor blade.

He cut one side of the waist-band of the pair of shorts. With that cut the pair of shorts could be pulled up just to my buttocks.

"This is Mikuyu! You will get very thin in no time here," said the prison warder, threateningly again, as he cut the other side of the waist-band of the shorts.

With that extra cut, the pair of shorts could be pulled up just over my buttocks.

He threw the short-sleeved, collarless shirt at me. He ordered me to put it on. The shirt had a number written on it. The number was 3/75.

I was told to gather up my personal clothing and follow him upstairs. We went up to the office of their boss. The name of their boss was Mwambala. Many people said he was less brutal than his predecessors. Up there they took down my personal details and gave me two pieces of a thread-bare blanket. They took away my wrist-watch, tie-pin, loose coins, wedding ring and ten-kwacha banknote. They put all of them into a white envelope. They wrote

3/75 on the envelope and sealed it. That envelope was put in a safe. Then they put my suit, shirt, tie, belt, a pair of underpants, shoes and socks in a small white clothbag. They tied up the mouth of the cloth-bag. The number 3/75 was written on that bag as well.

With the formalities over, the officer in charge wagged his right-hand forefinger at me.

"My job is to keep you here," he said. "I did not arrest you. I do not know the reason or care about why you are here. Those who arrested you will come one day to order your release. Until that day comes you are in my hands. If you are going to be difficult for me, I shall be twice difficult for you. But if you are going to behave yourself, then you will experience no problems with me," he finished.

"Take him to Cell B!" he ordered his men.

I clutched my precious possessions of two pieces of a thread-bare blanket and followed the prison warder down the stairs. When he unlocked the door into the open courtyard he saw a group of sick prisoners. They were being led in for treatment in the punishment cell which served as a clinic. He banged the door closed and ordered me to hide myself in an adjoining room.

"No, don't bother," said his colleague, "he is going to Cell B and they are from Cell B. It does not matter if they see each other."

That was the first lesson I learnt. Once in Mikuyu Prison, you were not supposed to know who was in the next cell. Strenuous efforts were made to ensure that there was no communication between the inmates of one cell and those of another. Your brother could be in the next cell but you would never get to know it for years.

He led me out into the courtyard and immediately turned right. He pulled back the bolt of a thick wooden door. He opened it for me.

That was the second lesson I learnt. Under no circumstances was a prisoner allowed to touch a door. He could be shot dead on sight. The mere act of touching the door was an attempt to escape. Such an attempt was punishable by an instant shoot-to-kill order.

He pushed me in and closed the door behind me. In front of me was a large number of men sitting down on the bare concrete ground. Many more were inside the cell itself.

My unexpected appearance was received with mixed feelings. First, because there were sixty-eight people in a cell which was designed to hold no more than twenty. Secondly, because my physical appearance cast doubts in the minds of some of the prisoners. They thought that I was not a genuine prisoner but a plant by the Special Branch.

"Look at him. He is well-fed. He must have been a member of the ruling clique. He has come to spy on us," I overheard someone whispering to another inmate at a corner.

It was painful for me to realize that some of them thought of me as a spy.

The Nyapala received me warmly. He was Mr Mhango. He was in merely because he was a cousin to Kanyama Chiume, an ex-Minister who had fled to Tanzania. He took me inside the cell and gave me a place to live on. It was no more than seventeen inches wide. Being broad-shouldered was a distinct disadvantage. We lay next to each other on the bare concrete floor like sardines in a can. There were three rows of us. Someone had his head against the wall and his feet on the crown of your head. You had your feet on the crown of the head of another man. There was no space to turn to. And there was no space in between. The tall ones had a special problem with their legs. We developed corns on the ankles, elbows and spine where they rubbed against the concrete floor.

The blankets, as well as the prison uniform, were heavily infested with thick, black lice. The only consolation was that, unlike the cell in Zomba Prison, we had no bucket. There was a flush toilet at the corner but water was a problem. The toilet was used until it was nearly full. Then it was flushed. Sometimes that kind of flushing never worked because the pipe was blocked. In that event one of us dipped his own arm and used his fingers to break whatever lump was blocking the pipe. The water in the cistern was very precious. It came in dribs and drabs. We drank it when our throats were cracking with thirst. The entire prison was served by a borehole and an electrical water pump. It was never adequate. Sometimes we went for a whole week or two without a shower.

After formally receiving me, the Nyapala and the others started to pump me for news. They were anxious to know about political developments outside. They also wanted to know about the health of Dr Banda. Pretty soon they all began to believe that I was a genuine prisoner. Two of the inmates in the cell were people I had known for a long time.

Dr Alifeyo Chilivumbo, a professor of sociology in the University of Malawi, had joined the faculty two years before I graduated. He had been detained because of his dress. Apparently, on graduation day, when Dr Banda was awarding degrees, in his capacity as the Chancellor of the University, Dr Chilivumbo had not put on his best suit for the occasion. However, at the graduation ball in the evening which Dr Banda never attended, Dr Chilivumbo was considered to have dressed well and better. That was considered an act of rudeness to the Head of State. The Special Branch men swooped down on Dr Chilivumbo immediately. They got him chained to the floor of CCI in Zomba Prison together with the condemned prisoners.

Every single day, the poor professor thought that he was going to be hanged. It was only much later, after a long spell on the death row, that the Special Branch sent the professor to Mikuyu Prison. There was one execution while he was there. Several people he had become used to were gone.

Another acquaintance was Kirby Mwambetania. He had been a year-mate of mine at the university. We graduated on the same day. He had joined the faculty and was a lecturer. He was picked up mainly because he was from the north.

I soon learnt that my number 3/75 meant that I was the third person to be detained in Mikuyu Maximum Security Prison in the year 1975. The first and second prisoners in 1975 were policemen.

In early January 1975, Dr Banda went to Zambia on a State Visit. As usual, a large crowd of dancing women and the entire senior section of the civil service, police, army and Cabinet Ministers were at Chileka Airport in Blantyre to see him off. As his long motorcade approached the airport grounds, two police officers tried to make way for it among the dancing women. The women took strong exception to that action. They complained loudly to another senior police officer that they were being prevented or stopped from dancing for their Nkhoswe Number One. That was sufficient. The two officers were bundled into a police landrover and driven straight to Mikuyu Prison. As far as the Special Branch was concerned, the two police officers had committed an act of treason. The allegation from the women was more than sufficient. There was no need for further investigations.

CHAPTER 10

A Son is Born

It became very clear to some of us that Dr Banda, and his Special Branch, were taking us for granted. The screws had been gradually but severely tightened. We were not allowed to receive visitors anymore. We were not allowed to write or receive letters from home. To some of us, worries about home were driving us crazy. Over half the inmates in Cell B were having very severe cases of high blood-pressure. At least one person was dying every month in our cell alone.

The food was becoming more and more terrible by the day. We were given Bonongwe for days on end. The *nsima* was cooked with flour from rotten maize. The aflatoxin in the maize made it taste bitter. The Bonongwe was simply mowed down with a sickle and dumped into a large drum for boiling. Sometimes they cooked it together with chameleons and some strange moths. It was revolting enough to see a dead chameleon in your metal mug.

I had gone to Mikuyu on 14 February 1975. What I could not stand anymore were the lice. In March, we organised a delegation to the Officer-In-Charge about the lice. The delegation suggested to him, quite peacefully and logically, that all the lice could be wiped out in one day by putting our blankets and clothing in boiling water. He agreed to the plan. Fortunately he did not have to refer it to the Special Branch. One morning, he had all our blankets soaked in a drum of boiling water. We took the blankets out, squeezed the water out and dried them in the sun. A couple of hours later, we wrapped ourselves with the dry blankets and soaked our prison uniforms in the boiling water. That day we slept peacefully. All the lice had perished. I left Mikuyu Prison two years later without seeing lice again. The Officer-In-Charge did the same thing cell after cell.

On 4 April 1975, I was called to the office for a visitor. It was my cousin, Stanley Wasi. He had braved the strong intimidation of the Special Branch, had come by bus all the way from Blantyre, and on foot from Zomba to Mikuyu. He brought me both good and bad news. The good news was that my wife had given birth to a baby son two days before, on 2 April, at Queen Elizabeth Central Hospital. The bad news was that soon after birth the baby had developed severe jaundice. He needed a blood transfusion. When my wife had insisted on calling for a doctor, and broke things to get attention, the hospital nurses thought that she had become insane. They got her rushed to Zomba Mental Hospital where she was locked up. The baby was all alone at Queen Elizabeth Central Hospital, with me, the father, in Mikuyu Maximum Security Prison and my wife, its mother, in Zomba Mental Hospital.

On arrival at Zomba Mental Hospital, my harassed wife was delivered into the hands of the Malawi Young Pioneers. They were running the hospital, in the absence of the Psychiatrist who had become an inmate of Zomba Prison. The Malawi Young Pioneers had very simple rules. They just clobbered any of the mad people who gave trouble. Then they got them chained down to hooks on the floor. When my wife was delivered to them, they tied her down to a chair before giving her an electric shock to the head. Who prescribed an electric shock, only God knows. They did not know how to use it and nearly succeeded in killing her.

My cousin Stanley left after fifteen minutes but I was a deeply disturbed man. I was very worried about my first-born baby son who was dying of jaundice in hospital in Blantyre. I was also very worried about my wife who was destroyed by an electric shock in Zomba Mental Hospital. I walked back to Cell B holding two rolls of toilet tissue which he had brought me as a gift. There were only three things which the prison authorities allowed us to receive from home. They were a tooth-brush, a tube of tooth-paste and rolls of toilet tissue. These were very precious possessions for us in prison.

When I told my fellow inmates that my wife had given birth to a baby son they unanimously christened him Mabvuto. I came to realise that every child, boy or girl, who was born while his or her father was in Mikuyu Prison, was called Mabvuto, meaning tribulations.

May 14 was fast approaching. The tension was high. We were all wondering if we were going to be released on that day. The tension was driving us crazy. We knew that if that day came, and passed, we would have to face another year. I was in that prison for only three months, but there were others who had been incarcerated since 1964, eleven years before. They had been taken to Nsanje Detention Camp. When that was closed down they were taken to the newly opened Dzeleka Detention Camp in Dowa. In 1973 when Mikuyu Maximum Security Prison was completed and Dzeleka was considered not secure enough, they were transferred to Mikuyu.

In that short time before 14 May, we had two suicide attempts. One morning a certain man from Mangochi, who had done eight years, calmly walked over to a column of the brick fence. He leaned his back firmly against a corner of the brick column. Then he leaned down as low as possible and swiftly raised his head to hit it against the sharp corners of the bricks. The first hit gave him a gash on the back of the head. Blood poured out all over his shoulders. He made two more swift hits before we pinned him down. He was bitterly disappointed that he had not succeeded in splitting his own skull in order to die. The prison warders came. They took him away to the punishment cell where he was stripped naked and chained to the floor. A week later he came back into the cell, a changed man.

Another suicide attempt was made by a man from Nsanje. This man had made a calculated move. He deliberately insulted a prison warder in order to be sent to the punishment cell. His plan succeeded. He was taken to the office of the Officer-In-Charge for trial. He admitted to the Officer-in-Charge that he had indeed answered back and insulted the junior prison warder. With that admission the man was sentenced to three days in the punishment cell.

The tradition was that, as soon as the sentence was passed, you had to run for your life. If you delayed, the prison warders rained their wooden clubs on you. They never stopped until the Officer-In-Charge blew his whistle. One minute of that savage beating was more than enough to kill you. The man knew everything. He fled downstairs on his own. He dashed into an open punishment cell and held the door against the warders who were chasing him. He was safe behind that door. They bitterly resented being cheated of their beating exercises by this clever prisoner.

He had other ideas and immediately set about to implement them. The security of the closed door was all he needed. Within minutes he used his fingernails to cut the pair of shorts of his prison uniform into strips of cloth. With those strips he made a strong noose. With that noose he hanged himself on the steel bars of the tiny window. He had nearly passed out when they saw him. Even in the punishment cell he was denied the chance to die in peace.

They opened the punishment cell hurriedly to cut him down. He was taken upstairs to the same kangaroo court for trial. He was swiftly sentenced to seven days for attempting the suicide. This time he was completely stripped of his clothing. Then they chained his legs together. Lastly, they chained his hands between his chained legs. That way he could not sit up or stand or even roll over. To crown it all they poured three pails full of cold water over him. The water never flowed out and he lay in it. This time they had sufficient time to beat him except that they nearly succeeded in killing him and thereby granting him his death wish. The first two days, they gave him no food or water to drink

On 12 May, we were locked up as usual at four o'clock. They went to the other cells to lock up the inmates there as well. Almost immediately thereafter, the entire establishment invaded our cell. The Officer-In-Charge was holding a sheet of paper. He was surrounded by his subordinates who wielded their truncheons menacingly.

"Anyone who hears his name must immediately pick up his blanket and walk out," he told us.

It was the long-awaited release.

We all cocked up our ears in anticipation, hoping against hope that our names would be on that sheet of paper. He began reading out the names. He folded up the sheet of paper after only four names. That was it. Another whole year to go in that hole of hell. Our hearts sank as we came to terms with the enormity of what had just happened. Our four colleagues were free men. They were on their way home. The door was closed, bolted and locked. We were still inside and behind the door.

That day I developed malaria. No one took me seriously. They suspected that it was just because I had missed the release. The following day the clinic officer did not report for duty. My temperature was rising steadily. It was cerebral malaria. On the third day I was dying. I knew deep down in my heart that it was a matter of hours, not days. I saw death, not with my eyes but in my eyes. The light was about to flicker out. It pained me to realise that, had I been a free man, I could have gone to my private doctor to get treatment easily. I could have even bought over-the-counter drugs to lower the temperature. Yet here I was, dying, just because I was denied access to drugs and treatment. In the afternoon of that day, I could not rise up anymore. After four o'clock they came to lock up my colleagues. They all walked in sullenly. The whole cell was quiet and deeply worried. They knew that they were about to see one of their own, me, die right in front of their eyes.

Suddenly a certain Mr Banda from Lirangwe could not take it any longer. He walked over to the door and started banging it with his right hand fist. He used all his strength.

"What are you doing?" said the worried prison guards as they came running with their guns at the ready.

"I am breaking down this door. We are all going home today," said Mr Banda with all the seriousness in the world. "You bastards want to see us die, one by one, to please your masters. Today is the last day. We shall not take that nonsense anymore. If you cannot take care of us we are going home. You can do whatever you want to do," said Mr Banda.

"What is all this about?" asked the worried warders.

"Sam Mpasu is dying here. For three days you have not given him any treatment because your man is busy drinking Kachasu."

"Hold on a minute, we shall get him," said the warders hurriedly.

True to their word, they opened the door to call me out. I could not walk out on my own. I was held by colleagues on either side. Fortunately, the man was sober when they found him. He thrust a thermometer into my mouth. When he took it out, he was visibly shaken. It was 41 degrees. He immediately filled up his syringe with procaine and jabbed me in the hip.

"That will do for today. I will see you tomorrow," he said.

I was too weak to talk to him or to anyone. I did not even care to ask if procaine was good enough for my cerebral malaria. I was inwardly relieved however when he did not insist that I be left alone in the punishment cell. My cell-mates held me on both sides and led me back to the cell.

No one in the cell fell asleep before midnight that day. They regarded the situation as still very serious. They expected me to die at any moment. I fell asleep but did not expect to see the morning. I told the Almighty God, in a short prayer in my heart, that if that was the day and the moment he had appointed for my departure from this world, could he please kindly forgive me all my sins and receive me in heaven. I thought of my newly born baby son, all alone in the hospital, like an orphan. I thought of my wife, at the tender mercies of the Malawi Young Pioneers, in the Zomba Mental Hospital. I looked at the seventy or so other inmates in Cell B. All of them had similar experiences. I thought of hundreds of the others in Cells A, C and D; all of them going through this unbearable anguish with their families. And what for? I failed to answer that question because it boiled down to Dr Hastings Kamuzu Banda's irrational and cruel dictatorship.

I was as surprised as everyone when I woke up in the morning. My body felt light. The temperature had dropped. The only problem was that I was very weak and had no appetite. In fact the taste of food made me vomit.

The door of the yard brick fence was opened suddenly.

"Only three from this cell including the one who was sick yesterday," the clinic warder said that morning.

Two people sprinted out but he held the door open for me. I got out of the cell. I was very surprised that I could walk out on my own.

That day, a certain person who had come to visit a relative, saw me by mistake and recognised me. I do not know him or her but when the person went home, they spread the story that I had died in prison. The rumour reached my home village in Ntcheu. My family adamantly refused to hold funeral rites unless they saw my dead body. The same rumour eventually reached my wife in Zomba Mental Hospital. She became very agitated. Fortunately, the government had been offered the services of a French doctor by that time. They had withdrawn the Malawi Young Pioneers. Very early in the morning, my wife slipped out of the Mental Hospital and started to walk along the road towards Blantyre.

Within an hour the word was out that a lady mental patient had escaped. The police were out in full force looking for her. They were worried about her because she was a foreigner. The Ethiopian Foreign Ministry in Addis Ababa had started to embarrass the Malawi Embassy with awkward questions about their national. The police found her at Seven Miles. To their credit, they did not use force. They brought her back to the Mental Hospital but that gave the French doctor the opportunity he had been looking for. He sat down with the police officers.

"This lady is not mentally disturbed or mad. I am not keeping her here. You have created a situation which convinces her that her baby was killed at birth and her husband has been killed in prison. It is up to you to prove to her that her baby is alive and her husband is alive," he lectured them.

At Queen Elizabeth Central Hospital in Blantyre an ambulance was hurriedly prepared. Two nurses brought my baby son to Zomba Mental Hospital. Fortunately, Dr John Chiphangwi had done the blood transfusion the same day my wife had been taken away. This was at considerable risk to his own job for not having left a "rebel's" child to die. The baby was alive and well, and big.

80

The problem was me.

The Special Branch had known that I was very sick but not yet dead. The rumour about my early death made them a bit uncomfortable. They wanted to use my wife to refute the rumour but they could not let her see me in the condition I was in. I was very thin and haggard. They feared that my wife could use whatever international connection she had to spill the beans about the living conditions at Mikuyu. The last thing they wanted was Amnesty International, or some other body, blowing the whistle on their abuse of human rights.

As soon as my wife saw the baby, she totally refused to be separated from him. That action earned her immediate release from the mental hospital. The same ambulance took her and the baby back to Queen Elizabeth Central Hospital in Blantyre. She collected her clothing and the baby's nappies from the maternity ward. The same ambulance took her to Soche where she had been living with my aunt, Stanley's mother. Before she left that maternity ward, she learned a few things from some of the nurses. They were very pleased to see her again, after two months.

The first story was that several curious people had gone to the maternity ward to have a close look at my baby. All along, these people had suspected that I was impotent and that was why I had married at thirty years old. My marriage to a foreigner, who could not be expected to disgrace me by spreading stories of my uselessness in bed, had been another proof for them. They went away convinced that I was not impotent because the baby resembled me more than it resembled its mother.

Another story she learned was that the baby had been very popular for another reason. Several people had actually asked the hospital authorities for permission to adopt it.

"This baby has no parents. Let us take him away to look after him," they said.

This made the hospital authorities very worried that the baby would be stolen. They beefed up security in the ward.

The third story she learned was that the baby was named Joseph and was already responding to that name. On further inquiry, she learnt that, one day in the morning, the harmless baby was crying a lot and none of the nurses on duty attended to him. A Zimbabwean nurse who was working at the hospital at that time heard the cries of the baby from far as she came in for her morning shift. She was disgusted with the attitude of the Malawian nurses.

"Why are you not attending to that crying baby?" she had asked.

"Why should we bother when his father has rebelled against Dr Banda?" she was answered. "He is the child of a rebel."

For the Zimbabwean nurse this was crass politics at its worst. She could not understand why the political views of its father had anything to do with the innocent baby.

"I am giving him a name today," the Zimbabwean nurse said resolutely. "His name is Joseph."

"But you cannot do that; he is not your baby," she was told vehemently by the Malawian nurses who were put to shame.

"Joseph was rejected and sold off into slavery by his own brothers. Here you are, Malawians, rejecting an innocent Malawian baby. His name is Joseph," she said firmly as she changed the baby's nappies and gave him a bottle-feed.

It was during the second week of June when the Special Branch allowed my wife to come and show me the baby. On that day, as usual, I was taken by surprise when the door was suddenly opened and my name called out. I suspected it was a visitor for me. My cell-mates held each other up to reach the ledge of the tiny windows at the top and peeped out. They saw my red Fiat 850 Sports Coupe outside the prison fence. I hurried to borrow a shirt because mine was all rags.

The prisoner was always the first to enter the visiting room. Then the visitors were allowed in. The warder always stood between them.

She walked in, beaming a smile and holding the big baby. I could not kiss her or hug her. I could not hold the baby. She turned his face for me to see him. It was during that time she told me about the ordeal at the mental hospital and the stories at the Queen Elizabeth Central Hospital. I told her that the name of the baby

82

was going to remain Joseph. We had no such name in my family or in hers. That did not matter.

When the visit was over, I told her to go and sell off our refrigerator to realise some money for the two of them. I went back to my cell holding six rolls of toilet paper in three colours, a tube of tooth-paste and a tooth-brush.

CHAPTER 11

The Funny Cases

Just like in Zomba prison, some of the allegations which many members of my cell had been imprisoned for were unbelievable. There was also plenty of evidence that the system was perfectly capable of destroying its own sons.

A tragic case was that of Sweetman Kumwenda. He had risen through the ranks of the Malawi Police Force and would have been the first Malawian to head it. A sudden and unexpected turn of events saw all the top eight Malawian police officers, including Mr Kumwenda, forced into immediate retirement. The ninth, Mr Kamwana, took over as the first Malawian to head the entire police force. Although they were forced into retirement, they were given jobs in various parastatal organisations. Sweetman Kumwenda did not last long in his. He was swept into Mikuyu Prison.

The great irony is that Sweetman Kumwenda had spent nearly all his time in the Special Branch. He used to tell us hair-raising stories about the murders and attempted murders he had done for and on behalf of Dr Banda.

"Now he repays me by locking me up here like this!" he would often lament pitifully.

One day he told me about the trouble they had in bagging a certain tall Trade Unionist called Chisiza. They got him in his office, in Limbe, in broad daylight. They used their wooden truncheons to knock out his kneecaps and elbows into numbness. Then they bent him double, alive, and shoved him into a sack. But he was too tall for the sack. Eventually they squeezed him in anyway and tied up the sack's mouth. He was crying uncontrollably, like a baby, for mercy. He appealed to Mr Kumwenda, whom he knew personally, but his fate was sealed. Mr Kumwenda put duty first. Their problem was how to take him to the Shire River because police road-blocks, manned by white police officers, were all over. It was Sweetman Kumwenda's brilliant idea that they use a police landrover, rather than a plain vehicle, because it would not be searched at the road-blocks. His plan succeeded. The police landrover was not searched. The human sack was thrown into the Shire River at Mpatamanga Bridge, on the old road to Zimbabwe, after Chileka Airport. The poor man was still crying for mercy when they dumped him into the river.

Another day he told me of a plan he had hatched to kill Henry Chipembere in Tanzania. He fled Malawi and pretended to have fallen out with Dr Banda. In Tanzania he managed to fool everyone. They all believed him. The critical day came when they eventually allowed him to enter Mr Chipembere's house for an audience. He was not searched and had his pistol ready to shoot Mr Chipembere on sight. He sat there in the sitting room waiting for Mr Chipembere to come out. Mr Chipembere unexpectedly refused to come out, of whatever room he was in, to meet him. Afraid that perhaps his sinister plot had been uncovered, Sweetman Kumwenda left the house in a hurry. He fled back to Malawi. He failed to get whatever prize Dr Banda had promised him.

It was Sweetman Kumwenda, by his own account, who had recommended to Dr Banda that a new maximum security prison for political prisoners should be built in Zomba, close to the police headquarters and the army headquarters. Dzeleka, he had told Dr Banda, was too far in Dowa in the Central Region and would be indefensible in the event of a massive jail-break. Mr Kumwenda was entrusted with the job of building such a maximum security prison. He had gone to South Africa and to Ghana to borrow architectural plans. It was he who had supervised the construction of Mikuyu Maximum Security Prison until it was ready for occupation. Then he was unexpectedly retired and subsequently arrested. Ironically, he became the first inmate of a prison he himself had built for others. The story of Mr Kumwenda reminded me of the story of Haman in the bible. When the escorted trucks of political prisoners arrived at Mikuyu from Dzeleka, in

1973, Sweetman Kumwenda had already been the sole occupant of Cell B and of the whole of the prison.

Unfortunately for Mr Kumwenda, he developed sores on his legs. They were in the form of painful scabs. He became progressively weak. All they gave him was a white cream to rub over the sores. In the end, when he was almost finished and very weak, he was taken from Mikuyu to Zomba Prison where he died. He was still a political prisoner.

Another sad spectacle was that of two brothers. They were both young and unmarried, Don and Albert Kwizombwe from Blantyre. Don had been working for the Malawi Broadcasting Corporation as an engineer. The Malawi Broadcasting Corporation had sent him for attachment to the BBC in London. As soon as he had left for London, office politics vanquished him. His enemies in the MBC spun out a story to the Special Branch to the effect that he had been monitoring Voice of America broadcasts. As far as the Special Branch was concerned, monitoring for the Voice of America meant spying for Americans. A polite message was sent to the BBC asking Don Kwizombwe to return immediately for a promotion which had been occasioned by a sudden vacancy. Don was met by the Special Branch at Chileka Airport. He was taken to jail right away.

His young brother Albert was a book-keeper in Grain & Milling Company in Limbe. He too became vanquished by office politics. An enemy of his in the company spun out a story to the Special Branch to the effect that Albert had been bad-mouthing the Malawi Government for having detained his elder brother. They jumped on him too. The two young brothers made the rounds of Chichiri Prison, Zomba Prison, Maula Prison, Dzeleka Prison and eventually Mikuyu Prison, a total of five years each, without trial. They were the sons of a widow.

Then there was this illiterate villager from Mangochi. As a teenager he had secured a labourer's job at Yiannakis Fisheries which Dr Banda forfeited and renamed Malawi Fisheries. On the way to his job, along a footpath one morning in 1965, he was confronted by the security forces. They bundled him into a landrover. Neither his employers nor his family knew what had befallen him. After Zomba prison he ended up at Dzeleka. By 1973, he had done eight years, when the Special Branch discovered him. The Special Branch were transferring all the political prisoners from Dzeleka Prison to Mikuyu Prison when, to their embarrassment, they discovered that they had no record of him at all. Instead of releasing him forthwith, they opened a file on him. They sent him to Mikuyu, along with the others, as a dangerous political prisoner. When I went to Mikuyu in 1975 he was doing his eleventh year in prison. The young teenager had become a man.

One afternoon we received George Trataris in Cell B, a scion of a prominent Greek family in Blantyre. His family had been pioneers in the bakery business in Malawi and had been instrumental in helping many other Greek families to settle into tobacco farming in Namwera, Mangochi and other districts. They had restructured and consolidated their bakery business. They called it Associated Bakeries. It had modern branches in Blantyre, Lilongwe and Mzuzu. He had over three-thousand head of cattle at his farm at Makhanga in the Lower Shire. The mistake he had made was to continue holding a Malawi passport. When he flew out to Zambia one day, to look at the prospects of opening a good restaurant in Lusaka, he was trailed. He was arrested on return at Chileka Airport. He was hardly a week in Zomba prison when he saw one of his bakery's trucks on the road outside, repainted: "Press Bakeries".

"They have stolen my bakeries !" he screamed in shock.

True, Associated Bakeries in Blantyre, Lilongwe and Mzuzu had become Press Bakeries, as part of Dr Banda's business empire, Press Corporation. George Trataris was then promoted to a full-fledged, dangerous political prisoner and sent to join us in Cell B in Mikuyu Prison. When he was released two years later, he was broke. The bakeries had gone, the cattle were gone and his marriage was on the rocks. He was told that while in Lusaka he had been seen exchanging a greeting on the street with a Malawian "rebel".

Another heartbreaking story was that of Wilfred Katola, a prosperous building contractor. A self-made man, Mr Katola had built up his business from humble beginnings as a plumber. He was at the Ministry of Works in Blantyre, attending the opening of public tenders, when the Special Branch pounced on him. They took him straight to prison. Unknown to him, his wife was also pounced upon and taken to prison. She too did not know about his arrest. All his business and personal assets, including trucks and cars, bedsheets and forks in his Lilongwe flat, tractors at the farm, personal clothing in the house were sent to Downs Auction Floors in Limbe for sale by auction. All the money went to the Malawi government. His wife had been running a grocery shop in Nkolokosa. All her groceries including packets of washing soap, were sent to the auction and sold off. His business offices in Blantyre were forfeited and given to the Malawi Bureau of Standards as its headquarters.

On the day of their arrest, no one told the children in Zingwangwa New Lines. The children were on the verandah at dusk, locked out of their own home by the police. A clandestine message was sent to his old mother in Ntcheu. She defied fate, got on a bus and collected the children back to the village. When he came out of Mikuyu Prison two years later, Mr Katola was not only a penniless man but was still under the provisions of the Forfeiture Act. This meant that any gift he would receive, or money he would make, belonged to the government. An envious man had told the authorities that Mr Katola was just a front for the "rebels" in Lusaka and his money was theirs. That was sufficient for the drastic action they took. They did not prove anything but that did not matter. Mr Katola got nothing back.

Another example of the system devouring its own sons was furnished by five functionaries of the Malawi Congress Party. They ran the party's branch of the Copperbelt in Zambia. These expatriate Malawians in Zambia were staunch supporters of Dr Banda's politics. They held prominent positions in the external branch of the Malawi Congress Party on the Copperbelt. In 1972, they were selected by their own fellow members, as delegates, to represent Malawians in Zambia at the Annual Malawi Congress Party Convention in Malawi. They were seized on entry, by the Special Branch, at the border in Mchinji and sent straight to Dzeleka Prison. Apparently, a telegram had been sent ahead of them denouncing them as spies for "rebels". When Dzeleka was closed down as insecure in 1973, they were transferred to Mikuyu. In 1975, one of them, a Mr Mkandawire, developed a serious illness which was turning his dark skin into almost dark green. He died in the punishment cell. His body was wrapped in brown paper and taken away to Zomba. These five people, for all those years, were unable to tell their employers or families in Zambia that they were in prison in Malawi, without trial. Both their families and employers were probably denouncing them for their heartless desertion. The remaining four were released in 1977, five years later, without apologies or explanations. That was not uppermost in their minds. They were glad and grateful to be free.

Then we had James Chirwa, an old, convivial man we had nicknamed "Computer". Mr Chirwa had left Malawi at the age of nineteen, in the 1930s, for South Africa. He grew up there to be street-wise. When the African National Congress decided to fight apartheid with gunfire, James Chirwa threw himself into the fight. He had gone to Cuba, Algeria, China, Vietnam and other places for guerilla training. He used to tell us very entertaining stories on how they used to cross the mighty Zambezi River by walking on the river bed under the noses of the security forces. Sometimes he told us how they killed a person with bare hands, without giving the person a chance to shout. Other times he told us how they preserved their own urine and sieved it for drinking, as water, in desert conditions. He was a thoroughly trained guerilla fighter.

One day Mr Chirwa was disguised as a businessman on a train between Bulawayo and Plumtree. Unknown to him, someone had tipped the security forces. He was arrested and tried for all the sabotage work he had done in South Africa on previous trips. He was sentenced to death. He successfully appealed against the death sentence. It was reduced from death to twenty years. Then he disclosed that he was originally a Malawian, and therefore the crime of treason could not apply to him. He appealed against the conviction, with limited success. The sentence was reduced from twenty years to twelve years. He was sent to Robben Island, to join his friend, Nelson Mandela, in breaking rocks at a quarry.

In 1976, his twelve years were over, with remission for good behaviour. He was taken to Johannesburg where he was immediately served with deportation orders, as a foreigner. He was put on a plane for Malawi, a country he had not known for over forty-years. On arrival at Chileka Airport, the Special Branch met him. They whisked him away to join us in Cell B in Mikuyu.

"I have never broken any Malawi law and I served my sentence in South Africa. Why is the Malawi Government putting me in jail?" this old man used to complain incessantly.

He was so confident that, one day, South Africa would be free and his friend, Nelson Mandela, would lift the deportation order for him to go back to South Africa.

CHAPTER 12

Life in Prison

By design, the inmates of Mikuyu Maximum Security Prison were not supposed to have any entertainment whatsoever. No provision was made for exercises, reading materials or a humble radio to listen to.

A simple bible from the Gideons was not available, let alone a koran. Books, magazines and newspapers were all banned. We were expected to sit idly by, all day every day, week after week, month after month and year after year. Time weighed very heavily on us. Boredom was part of the punishment. Dr Hastings Kamuzu Banda, the architect of this type of punishment, called it "rotting". We were rotting with boredom both mentally and physiologically. Several of us had muscles atrophying. Night blindness usually set in on most of us. The problem miraculously cleared off when they gave us the dry, rotting, small fish called Matemba, one each. But that was a luxury we enjoyed only once after several months. All of us wished we were penal labour. At least we could have seen the sun regularly outside and the hard labour would have exercised our muscles.

Psychologically, it often became a matter of matching our wits against theirs. One thing they could not stop us from doing, even if they had wanted to, was our prayers. In our Cell B we had two religions only: Christianity and Islam. We made an amicable, internal arrangement with each other. The Moslems prayed during the mid-morning and the Christians prayed during the mid-afternoon. In the evenings both religions prayed, but one after the other.

We had no special place to pray. We used the same hard concrete floor we slept on. The preacher simply wrapped himself in an old blanket over his prison shorts. That was the cassock. He stood in front of us without a hymn book or bible and gave us a touching sermon. We alternated as preachers but on a voluntary basis. There was a full-fledged choir which lent dignity and flavour to the prayer service. I had never known that I was good at singing bass until I started singing in the choir of our prison cell.

It was amazing how some of the prisoners, after seven or eight years without seeing a bible or hymn book, could cite chapters and verses in the bible or sing a whole hymn, from memory. In fact our prayer service became infectious. The loud voices we made as we sang or preached wafted over the prison walls and fences, to the outside world. The wives and children of the prison staff left their houses in the evenings to come and lean against the security wire fence. They were anxious to get closer to us. They wanted to get every word we sang or uttered. Many of them walked back to their houses with troubled consciences. They told their fathers or husbands that they were in wrong jobs. Money was necessary but not at the expense of torturing the innocent people of God, they said. The husbands retorted that there were no alternatives as jobs were scarce.

Some of the marriages became decidedly unstable. The wives took advantage of every opportunity to go back to their own home villages. They stayed there for as long as possible. The prison staff themselves became prisoners of the community around them. They were sullenly ostracized by the people every time they passed through the villages for a beer-drink party. Some were actually beaten up. Quite often it was safer for them to move about without their prison staff uniforms on.

The Moslems in our Cell B were lucky; they had two Sheikhs as fellow political prisoners. The only problem they had was one of hierarchy. The older and the senior Sheikh was gentle, unassuming and courteous in spite of his status. The younger one was a real radical. He was also blessed with a short temper. I remember at one time he had been spoiling for a fisticuff fight with one of the prison warders. Unfortunately for him, the prison warders had been looking for a suitable opportunity to tame him.

On this particular day, we were coming from the showers. The younger Sheikh deliberately insulted the prison warder he had targeted. When the warder reciprocated in kind, the Sheikh moved closer to knock him down. The warder ducked the fist but grabbed the Sheikh's genitals instantly. One violent pull and the Sheikh was flat on his back, groaning with unbearable pain. That was the end of the one-sided fight. A whistle was blown. The rest of the warders came running. Their quarry was already down on the ground as they pounded him with their wooden truncheons and kicked him mercilessly with their thick boots. Half conscious, he was dragged for a kangaroo trial in the office of the Officer-in-Charge. He was sentenced to seven days in the punishment cell. Three days without food or drink, the remaining days on half ration and four pails of cold water over him. He was a subdued and changed man when he was released from the punishment cell. His radicalism had evaporated.

Another problem the Moslems had was water. It was absolutely necessary for them to wash themselves before prayers. Yet they had no access to water. They used the water in the cistern of the flush toilet. A plateful of that water was passed around. The pretence of washing was symbolically sufficient.

It was the first time for me to live with Moslems so closely. I was fascinated by the tenacity they showed to their beliefs. The fastidiousness with which they performed every ritual was quite gripping. When they wanted to face Mecca they faced Mecca. The Sheikh pointed out where Mecca was in the prison cell. That was sufficient. His word was law and could not be disputed. They chanted their songs and sang their prayers so dutifully that it was quite an entertainment in itself, to those of us who did not understand much about it. Sometimes they sat cross-legged on the floor, touching their beads in silent prayers. Sometimes they knelt on their knees and periodically touched their foreheads on the bare concrete floor. It is a pity that I never understood anything because they used the Arabic language and to some extent the Yao language. What I understood very clearly was that bodily cleanliness was a central theme for their spiritual purity.

We always begged our relatives to bring us coloured toilet

tissue rolls on their visits. The coloured toilet tissue rolls we cherished so much were not entirely for the toilet. By using the remains of maize-flour porridge as glue, we pasted together coloured boards for games. We made chess, monopoly, snakes-and-ladders, draughts, cards and others. There was no shortage of this type of glue. Maize flour porridge was the only breakfast we were given. We ate it day after day, week after week and year after year. It had no sugar and we used no spoons.

Lumps of *nsima* were hand-pressed into various shapes dictated by our imagination. We dried the pieces in the sun away from the prying eyes of the prison staff. The kings, queens, knight, castles and pawns we made were for chess and dice for monopoly. As soon as the door was closed behind us, we played the games. Sometimes we played against each other as keenly as if it was an international tournament. Sometimes there was more joy to be had in watching others play.

It was all against the prison regulations but who cared? The voices we raised in excitement often gave us away. Quite often, out of the blue, the Officer-in-Charge would burst in on us the following morning, surrounded by his men, for an inspection. The inspections were so thorough that, no matter how ingeniously we tried to conceal our treasured games, the prison officers always found them. They even unfolded the blankets and shook them down. With broken hearts, we saw our cherished games carted away for destruction. We really felt stunned after every inspection. The inspections were sometimes as regular as twice a week. After recovering from the shock of the losses, we always started to make the games again as soon as the prison officers turned their backs on us. We had nothing more to loose but the boredom.

Another feat we had always won was communications with the inmates of the other cells. By design, the inmates of one cell in Mikuyu Prison were not supposed to know who was in the next cell. You could not know if your brother was also a political prisoner in the adjoining cell. We beat that system. We developed ingenious communication systems which enabled us to communicate with the inmates of all the other cells. Quite often under the noses of the prison officers. We knew the names and backgrounds of every new arrival in the prison and in every cell. We also shared news of the outside world. New arrivals from Zomba Prison always brought us the latest news of the outside world.

We were not restricted by time either. We could communicate in broad daylight with the inmates of other cells while we were taking showers. We also communicated with them in the evenings after lock-up.

The systems we used were very simple. First we checked if the guards on duty were from the south, centre or north. This enabled us to gauge which Malawi languages they understood or spoke. If he was from the north we knew that he could not speak Yao or Lomwe. If he was from the south we knew that he could not speak Nkhonde or Tonga. If he was from the centre we knew that he could not understand any of the marginal languages of the north or the south. Sometimes we got bogged down when we suspected that they knew the languages we wanted to use. In that case we resorted to foreign languages. We used German, French, Swahili, Bemba, Shona or Zulu, but never English. They could always understand English.

Almost invariably none of them had ever travelled outside the country, while the prison cells were teeming with intellectuals, academics, civil servants and diplomats who had worked or studied in other countries. We were fluent in several foreign languages.

Whenever we had a message to communicate in the evenings, we deliberately raised our noises or sang hymns. Then one of us would stroll over to the connecting wall between the two cells and lean his back against it. He sent a telegram to the other cell by hitting his heel against the wall a number of times. That telegram alerted the other side that there was a message to be received. They sent a reply in the same form. Then we would ask for a Yao speaker or some other language just above the din of the noises we made. That way, lengthy conversations, shouted through the wall, were carried out and the prison officers were none the wiser.

We never threw away the thin slices of bar soap we were given as bath soaps. We used the slices as letters for correspondence. We wrote the message by scratching the thin slice of soap. After wrapping it up in a few pieces of toilet tissue paper we threw the harmless-looking piece over the fence into the yard of the next cell. Sometimes we simply tucked the message in an obscure crevice in the shower-room. Then we told the other inmates, through the unfamiliar language, where they would find it when they went for a shower.

All these things were extremely risky. We were not allowed to do anything of the sort. Once caught, retribution was swift and severe. The suspect was unceremoniously hauled off to the office of the Officer-in-Charge for a kangaroo trial, which was invariably followed by a brutal beating and several days in the punishment cell.

The only privilege they allowed us occasionally was a couple of blunt razor-blades for each cell. The bluntness did not matter. There were some among us who had developed expertise in handling those blunt razor-blades or sharpening them against the concrete floor, to give a passable hair-cut. Our visitors used to wonder if we had visiting barbers. With such presentable hair-cuts, our visitors went away mistakenly believing that we were well-looked after. Even our beards were trimmed. This privilege was rare, perhaps once a month. On their own, the prison staff would decide to give us the blunt razor-blades. The razors were given in the morning and taken away in the afternoon. There was always a scramble to get a hair-cut that day. Once the opportunity for a hair-cut was lost, it could be another month. A lot depended on cultivating a friendly relationship with the experts in the cell.

We had tea only once a year, on Christmas Day. All they did was boil a pailful of water, throw in a handful of coarse tea leaves and a handful of brown sugar. The contents were stirred. We then lined up in front of the pail for the annual luxury of half a mug of steaming tea. That half mug of tea made all the difference between an ordinary day and Christmas Day.

When green maize was in season, the Officer-in-Charge could

use his discretion to have some boiled and given to us. The nearby prison was the source. The penal labour prisoners in the other Mikuyu Prison tilled the farm and harvested the maize. If we got a cob each, that day we felt like having dined out at a luxury hotel.

Very occasionally they gave us meat. It was as infrequent as once in four months. Even then it was no more than one small piece per person. Whoever went shopping made sure to get us bones. It really was what is called dog-meat but we celebrated. We saved and concealed every bone. By sucking at the bone or dipping the lump of *nsima* into the gruel, we finished the plate of *nsima*.

We had experts who smashed the bones against the concrete floor. The pieces were then continually rubbed against the concrete floor into various shapes. Out of the pieces, a beautiful hair comb could be made by using the yarn pulled out of the old blankets. Those miniature combs worked. We looked presentable with combed hair. The experts could make even needles out of the bone pieces. We used the needles to knit our prison numbers on our prison blankets, for easy identification.

Whenever a new political prisoner joined us in our cell, we received him very warmly. A new arrival always looked thoroughly dazed. Mikuyu was a place where every ounce of reassurance was necessary. We encouraged the new fellow to look at life with more optimism. We made him believe that so long as there was breath in his body the possibility of release was always there. The most reassuring people were those who had done ten years or more and were still alive. The fear of Mikuyu Maximum Prison was more outside than inside.

A certain young man, who was a graduate Civil Engineer, was nearly killed one day. His name was Chris Gondwe. He was on the back of an open truck, with others, being taken from Zomba to Mikuyu prison. Scared of Mikuyu prison he decided to take his chances and jumped off the moving truck. The escort warders raised their guns to shoot him dead. Fortunately, he stayed put where he had landed. His foot was badly sprained and twisted. They picked him up and took him back to Zomba prison for treatment. After a couple of weeks they brought him to Mikuyu again. He was limping but quite humorous about it.

We always pumped the new arrivals for news of the outside world. We extracted more through expert questioning. If there was anything worthwhile in the news, we always relayed it to the other cells, through the telegraphy we had developed.

Just like in the communities outside, the occurrence of death in the cells always hushed us into an angry silence. Angry because of the needlessness of those deaths. The deaths occurred because we were deliberately neglected as far as medical services were concerned. The prison staff quite often seized the opportunity to wound us further. When we were all dazed by the death of a fellow inmate, they taunted us to our faces. They said that we were all there to die off.

"You are all going to be finished off here," they said, "to teach you a lesson about the folly of opposing Dr Banda."

When an inmate woke up with a terrible backache in the morning, and sought medical treatment, he became the butt of jokes. The prison staff roared off into laughter

"You are just missing your wife", they said, as they turned the poor fellow away, without treatment.

It was a cruel joke, especially to a man who has had no access to his wife for ten years.

Whenever one of us died, we relayed the news to all the other cells through the secret telegraphy. In the evening, every cell held a funeral service in honour of the departed. The sermons largely reflected the desperateness and helplessness we were in. The loud prayers implored the Almighty God to deliver us from the hands of the cruel Pharaoh, who was grinding us to death, just as He had delivered the down-trodden Israelites, from their own Pharaoh in Ancient Egypt.

In summer the water-table dropped. The electric water pump failed to get any water from the borehole. This meant extra hardship for all of us. They reserved water only for cooking and we went for weeks without a shower. We sweated profusely during the day and during the night, because of the humidity. We got hydrated and there was not much water to drink, let alone for a shower to wash away the sweat. The water in the cistern of the flush toilet became very precious for drinking. The cell was hell. It was very warm. The hot breath of seventy or eighty people, crammed into a single open room, exacerbated the problem. The tiny windows at the top never helped.

As if that was not enough, mosquitoes were there in swarms. The grim walls carried plenty of evidence of our own valiant war against the mosquitoes. Smudges of human blood were all over where we had squashed the mosquitoes after they had filled themselves with our blood.

Sometimes nature came to our assistance. After going for weeks without a shower, a sudden downpour of rain was very welcome indeed. We hurriedly tossed off our prison uniforms and dashed into the rain to wash ourselves. The spectacle of dozens of grown-up, stark-naked men jostling in the rain was laughable if it was not so tragic. A sudden downpour often meant a sudden stop. When the rain stopped before the soap was washed off, there was an extra problem. It was a place without such basics as bath-towels. Once again, the water in the cistern of the single flush toilet came to our assistance. A small plate of water from there was sufficient to complete the bath.

Like several other inmates, I developed a peculiar health problem. I had a permanent cold. I was bothered daily with a running nose. This is bad enough when one has a handkerchief but its inconvenience is nightmarish when one is in prison without a handkerchief, a tissue or anything like it.

There were many others who developed respiratory diseases or high blood pressure. The evenings were always hell for such people. The closeness of so many people in one room generated extra heat from our breaths. Fresh air from tiny windows at the top was totally inadequate. Quite regularly, some of the inmates collapsed suddenly and made uncontrollable, loud, guttural noises as they desperately fought for breath. We always rushed over during such emergencies to fan the victims with our prison shirts. That way, we managed to save some of them from sudden deaths, right in front of our eyes.

Fisticuff fights were not uncommon either. An inmate who had set himself apart at a corner was the most dangerous. The chances were that he was buried in thoughts, worried sick about the fate of his family. Such a person had to be given a wide berth because a sudden disturbance was more likely to anger him, and make him fly at you with a punch on the nose. Even a simple innocuous joke could easily cause a problem, if made carelessly. In a way we were all mentally disturbed people in that horrible place. It was an underworld, a replica of hell on earth, which was created by man for man.

Malawi was slow in banning DDT, the chemical which was widely used for the protection of crops. It used to happen that the prison authorities gave us the weevil-infested but DDT-treated pegion-peas. No matter how hard the kitchen washed off the chemical, its residues gave us trouble. The whole cell suddenly developed tummy problems. The bowels churned and felt like someone was slicing them into pieces. Then the purging started. The problem was badly compounded by the inadequacy of the toilet. There was only one toilet at an open corner for a cell which had over seventy inmates. Squatting on the toilet seat, in full view of all those people, was difficult enough but we pulled our prison shirts over our faces to conceal the feelings of shame. Meanwhile, there was this long queue of grown-up people who were anxiously waiting for the same toilet seat. Some of them were barely controlling themselves, while the others were overcome by the purging, as they awaited their turn on the toilet seat.

A favourite pastime we had was telling each other dreams and seeking interpretations. Some of the interpretations were distressing enough. If you dreamt about monkeys, you were told that they were false friends and, most likely, your wife was having an affair at home. If you dreamt about dogs chasing you, you were told that the police had a serious charge against you. If you dreamt about a woman you know being pregnant, it meant that she was having trouble. If you dreamt that you were on an aeroplane which was failing to take off, or actually took off but crashed, it meant that your chances of release were thwarted. If you dreamt that a big lion was chasing you, and you escaped by climbing a tree only to see the tree taper downwards to within reach of the lion, it meant that your problems with Dr Banda were serious enough to merit execution. If you dreamt about a live mud-fish, it meant that your relative had died at home. If you dreamt that you were swimming vigorously and happily, it meant that you were on top of your problems.

Sometimes it was more prudent not to seek interpretations for a terrible dream. A serious depression could follow. Once, I dreamt that I was taking off a T-shirt, only to see a similar one on my body and so on, as I took off one after another. I was told that I had a baby son. It was true. He was born that day.

CHAPTER 13

The Cloth and The University

Malawian ladies may not have much money for shopping, but they know fashion when they see it. They dress very attractively and fashionably, without spending a fortune. During the last half of 1975, a Japanese textile firm produced a *kanga* cloth which had the head of an African young woman, adorned with plaited hair. An enterprising Asian young man working for Robray Limited, foam-mattress makers in Limbe, saw a fortune in that cloth. He obtained commission rights throughout Malawi. It sold like hot cakes.

Suddenly a rumour surfaced. Whether it was started by the Special Branch, or someone else, is neither here nor there. The rumour, which angered Dr Banda terribly, was that the face on the cloth was that of a girl-friend of ex-Cabinet Minister Kanyama Chiume, who had fled into political exile in Tanzania. According to Dr Banda's warped way of reasoning, any Malawian who bought or used that cloth was a supporter of Kanyama Chiume and, by extension, an underground enemy of Dr Banda himself. The implications of that reasoning became apparent instantly.

Thousands of women and girls who were seen putting on that cloth were summarily hauled off into jails without trial. By putting on that cloth, they had automatically become political enemies of Dr Banda and therefore became political prisoners. Those who had escaped the net, secretly poured paraffin on the cursed cloth, and burned it in the privacy of their bedrooms. They threw the ashes into the garbage bins at night. Even in the bin, they scattered the ashes away to remove any traces of evidence. Those who had no garbage bins tied up the cursed cloth into a ball, and tossed it into a pit latrine. Overnight, the cloth disappeared from view throughout Malawi. In the countryside, the dreaded Youth League combed the homes and meted out severe beatings before making arrests.

The jails were filled with dazed women and young girls who had never thought of themselves as politicians, let alone as political opponents of Dr Banda. The Asian young man was thrown into jail as well. However, being a holder of a British passport, he could not be detained as a political prisoner. He was put on the plane and deported. Fortunately, he had no shareholding in Robray Limited, which saved the company from the provisions of the Forfeiture Act.

The victimization campaign took absurd proportions. Peter Kalilombe, a respected and highly capable Permanent Secretary, was sacked. His wife, who was Matron of Queen Elizabeth Central Hospital, was also sacked. They had not bought or even seen the cloth. He was accused of having been the Permanent Secretary for Trade and Industry when the cloth was first imported. By the same warped reasoning, he was accused of having authorised its importation. His wife was sacked, merely because she was his wife. Telling Dr Banda that the ministry had no direct contact with imported commodities, and that only the Customs Department inspected goods, was like praying to a statue made of stone. His word was law and the law stood.

Kanyama Chiume was horrified to learn what was going on in Malawi, in his name. He issued a statement in exile denying any responsibility for the cloth. The Malawi Police Force were embarrassed. They sent a team to Japan to investigate. They found heaps of the cloth on the factory floor destined for Cameroon, Zaire, Congo, Nigeria, Ghana and Ivory Coast. They were told, to their faces, that the company had never heard of a man by the name of Kanyama Chiume. They were also told that the Japanese textile firm had commissioned the design of the cloth themselves. Shame-faced, the police delegation returned to Malawi. It was then that Dr Banda started to tone down his ranting against perceived political enemies at home. Many of the women were released. One of the poorest countries in Africa could afford to spend enormous amounts of money on such idiocies.

The Special Branch decided to move against the University of Malawi, specifically Chancellor College, and specifically the dons from the north. They were accused of flagrant nepotism in staff recruitment and student selection. The trick by the Special Branch was simple. They forged a letter from Kanyama Chiume. His forged signature was at the bottom of that letter. All they did was choose the addressee, jump on the plane at Chileka Airport and post the letter in Lusaka back to Malawi. They then intercepted their own letter at the Post Office and confronted the victim with it. Denial was impossible. The targeted victim was accused of having been corresponding treasonably with a "rebel", namely Kanyama Chiume.

It was through that way that the University was purged of the hated Northerners. Dr Peter Mwanza, the Principal of Chancellor College, which is the main campus of the University of Malawi, suddenly found himself behind bars in Zomba Prison. So did John Banda, the University Registrar. Other professors and lecturers followed suit, to such an extent that students were worried about who was going to teach them.

The chief informant of the Special Branch was a man in the college administration. It was he who decided which of his colleagues was going to go that week. The dons used to go to the college very early in the morning and watch him keenly as he got out of his car. If he looked scowling and frowning, they rushed to their telephones to describe every detail to their wives at home. They ended their conversations with a provisional farewell to the wives. If he came out of the car with a radiant and smiling face, they also rushed to the telephones to describe every detail to their wives. They too would smile that day, fortified with the knowledge that no one was going to be picked up that day.

It was a terrible situation which turned everyone into a nervous wreck. Living in constant and daily fear of being picked up was worse than actually being picked up. The uncertainty was more punishing than the certainty.

The consequence of Dr Banda's fulminations against the

humble cloth and the move by the Special Branch against the University of Malawi was that the jails were overcrowded. We had our fair share of the new arrivals at Mikuyu Maximum Security Prison.

Another consequence was that the nervousness of the political establishment made them tighten up security against those of us who were already inside. We were not allowed to receive visitors or letters any more. The food got worse. Brutality against us intensified. The overcrowding meant that hygienic conditions deteriorated. Fresh air for breathing, especially at night, was at a premium.

The Special Branch brought in a Police Photographer who spent several days taking photographs of us. We were made to hold a small, black plank, on which our prison-numbers were written in white chalk. We held the plank across the chest and he snapped us, one after another. Then he took a second snap from the side; a profile. According to a rumour, the Government had learnt of a conspiracy, by an outside organisation, to invade Mikuyu Prison and free all the political prisoners. According to another rumour, Dr Banda was going to be overthrown by his own ministers. We were all going to be released, as a goodwill gesture by the new rulers to the jubilant people of Malawi. After the euphoria, the Special Branch were then going to use the photographs to track us down and liquidate us, one by one. They then would blame the sympathisers of the overthrown Dr Banda for the mysterious deaths.

We never knew what was what but the photographs were real and the intensified suffering was real.

CHAPTER 14

The Hunger Strike

In early 1976 we heard stories of a presidential candidate in the United States of America by the name of Jimmy Carter. It was said that this man had brought a slogan of Respect For Human Rights to the presidential campaign. What was very exciting for us was the fact that he proposed to suspend American aid to African developing countries whose leaders oppressed their own citizens. That was enough to make some of us pray for the electoral success of Jimmy Carter. We hoped that Dr Banda would be forced to choose between keeping all of us in jail and foregoing the aid, or releasing us in order to receive the aid.

14 May 1976, Kamuzu Day, came and went. Only one person was released from the overcrowded Mikuyu Prison. The lucky man was the late Hon Alec Nyasulu, a former Member of Parliament, Cabinet Minister and Speaker of the National Assembly. He was a highly respected man but even he had ended up in jail.

What happened that day was the best news for me. But not everyone appreciated or understood my analysis. I was nearly punched on the nose that day by a fellow inmate from Mangochi. He was very angry to realise that he was starting his eighth year inside. I told him, quite frankly, that Dr Banda had painted himself into a corner by his failure to release us. He had failed to create room in prison for the many arrests his Special Branch were still making. The situation he had created was untenable, unless he did one of two things. He was either going to release lots of us long before the Kamuzu Day of the following year, or he was going to build lots of prisons for the overflow, long before the Kamuzu Day of the following year. My friend was not convinced.

Largely as a result of the deterioration in living conditions, many of us began to believe that life was not worth living. We began to believe that we were better off dead. We talked it over and over again, before we decided to stage the first ever mass hunger strike. We chose the day. The message was passed to the other cells, including the kitchen in Cell D. The response we got was very positive. We had some cowards among us, but we made it very clear to them that anyone who touched a plate of food that day would be dead, killed by us. Our reasoning was that Dr Banda would be so infuriated by the hunger strike that he would send his security forces to come and shoot us all dead. Short, sharp death at his hands would be preferable to the long and painful death which was taking us off, one by one, through atrocious living conditions.

The day came. Trays full of plates of maize-flour porridge were left, as usual, outside our cell gate. We looked at the plates sullenly. No one touched a plate that day. It was the same, cell after cell. Even those in the kitchen who had prepared it refused to eat it.

Pretty soon, the Officer-in-Charge came to assess the situation. We told him to go away. He did.

"You did not bring us here. You do not know why we are here. We want the one who sent us here," we told him firmly.

Within minutes, his boss, who was based at Zomba Prison, a Mr Mhango, turned up. He mistakenly thought we were striking for better food. He started making promises that he would give us groundnuts, more meat and more often, rice, tea, bread and so on. We told him curtly to go away. He did.

By mid-morning, they had realized that it was not a matter for the prison authorities anymore, but for the police itself. It was the kind of crisis they never had before. Many of us were prepared to kill or get killed that day. The situation was very tense. By midday, the political prisoners in the kitchen dutifully prepared lunch and brought the trays to our cell gates. No one touched it. They too did not touch their own food. All the prison warders, including their boss, were very nervous. They knew that they did not have enough bullets for all of us, if we decided to go for their throats.

They knew that it was going to be a messy massacre and some of them would be dead too.

Apparently, the Special Branch decided to use diplomacy rather than force. Focus Gwede himself came. He went from cell to cell. He was a humbled man who could not believe what was happening. Never, in the history of political detention in Malawi, had anything like that happened. What puzzled them more was how we had communicated and coordinated it all, to affect all the cells. He had a revolver in the inside pocket of his civilian jacket. He pleaded with us to follow the path of peace and negotiate our demands. We laid them down. He accepted all of them.

The diet improved immediately. We ate meat three times that week. All the letters they had been holding from our families were suddenly released to us to read. Our families started to visit us. What was even more significant was that he allowed us to write petitions to Dr Banda directly. I wrote one for myself and for four others. Two weeks later, I was called to the office together with the other four I had written for. Dr Banda had replied to our petitions. The Police Officer read the reply to us, quite sombrely. In his letter, Dr Banda thanked us for communicating with him and told us that he would look into our complaints. That, too, was unprecedented. Dr Banda had never replied to a political prisoner's letter before that day.

Three weeks later, in June, the Ministry of Works began digging the foundations for a new wing of cells at Mikuyu Maximum Security Prison. That wing was being built next to the office block and completely detached from all the other cells. The building activity was feverish. Within weeks the walls were up.

Totally unexpectedly, a review of our cases was started by the Special Branch itself. A certain Mr Mpemba, who was responsible for Mikuyu Prison in the Special Branch, interviewed all of us, one by one, and cell after cell. When it was my turn, he applied appeasement and bluster. He started by intimidating me. He pointed at the new wing which was hastily being erected.

"Do you see that building?" he asked me. "It is for unrepentant ring-leaders like you," he answered his own question.

Then he pulled out my file and browsed through it quickly.

"Sam," he said, "You have done nothing wrong to be here. You are innocent and should not have been detained at all. But there are some powerful people who want you inside. We obey orders. We cannot release you. Only God will release you, but do not do anything stupid which will prolong your stay here, unnecessarily," he said.

"Who are the powerful people?" I asked him.

"I cannot tell you. And you must not tell anyone else about what I have said here," he said fearfully.

Then he changed the subject and said how fortunate we all were to be detained by a civilized and humane leader, like Dr Banda, when our fellow political prisoners in Eastern Europe got their heads smoked while dangling from the ceiling where their legs were tied.

"Is that what you want to start doing here?" I asked him.

"No, no of course not. But the Police Force is large and you never know who might be in charge next time," he replied.

Lastly, he asked me if I had any special problem or complaint. I told him about my pre-molar tooth which had developed cavities and was giving me terrible pain every day. In fact my cheek was monstrously swollen at that time.

He jotted that down and promised to arrange for its early extraction. My interview was over. I went back to my cell. What surprised me was that my wife had stopped visiting me. In fact I never received any visit from any members of my family for a good part of that year. That gave me terrible worries. Little did I know that my dear, sweet and loving wife was pregnant from another man. My marriage was destroyed. It had become another casualty of Dr Banda's detention-without-trial. None of my relatives wanted to be the one to break the news of my wife's pregnancy to me.

CHAPTER 15

The Fall of The Mighty

During the last half of 1976, Malawi went through political changes which gave many people hope for a better life. Some went so far as to predict the advent of real personal freedom, throughout the country. Two personalities who had been closely identified with repression fell from grace that time. They were Focus Gwede, who was the head of the Special Branch, and Albert Muwalo, who was both the Secretary-General and Administrative Secretary of the Malawi Congress Party as well as Minister Without Portfolio. As Minister Without Portfolio he sat in the Cabinet and exercised considerable powers over several areas. They were not formal powers but he controlled access to Dr Banda. Whatever he recommended to Dr Banda was approved. Pretty soon he was wielding so much power over the Police and Immigration, without any ostensible authority to do so, that he was considered to be the real Minister of Interior rather than Dr Banda himself.

Albert Muwalo's personality was such that even his fellow Cabinet Ministers started to hold him in awe. None dared to cross him. In fact they started to pay homage to him in order to remain in his good books. He was ruthless enough to terminate the political career of any politician in the Cabinet, in Parliament and in the Party. If he wanted anyone picked up by the police, they were picked up. Failure to be granted an appointment by Mr Muwalo drove many people to distraction, for it meant the beginning of the end of one's political career, which was always tragic. I remember a certain politician who had driven all the way to Blantyre from Ntcheu, in order to explain himself out of trouble to Mr Muwalo. When Mr Muwalo refused to see him that day, he walked round the wire fence of the Malawi Congress Party headquarters office in Blantyre. He identified a suitable mango tree on which he intended to end his own life. He produced a rope and climbed the tree. Life was not worth living for him. Passersby saw him dangling from a branch of the tree as he fought for breath. They cut him down and saved his life.

Mr Muwalo was a Ngoni from Ntcheu. Focus Gwede was also Ngoni, but from Machinga. He had married a girl from Magola Village which was not far from Mr Muwalo's own home village. The connection of these two people with Ntcheu was enough to make all people from Ntcheu hated heartily in some quarters. This antipathy for Ntcheu Ngoni was largely misplaced and without foundation. Both Mr Muwalo and Mr Gwede were notorious for their lack of nepotism for fellow Ntcheu Ngoni. In fact they went out of their way to clobber anyone from Ntcheu, who became prominent by dint of his own effort, in any department or parastatal. I was a perfect example. They certainly did not lift a finger to save me from trouble. On the contrary, Gwede seemed to be very jubilant about getting me into jail.

In July that year, Malawi held a Trade Fair. For some unknown reason, Dr Banda failed to open the fair and instructed Mr Muwalo to do so on his behalf. Mr Muwalo imprudently digressed from economic affairs, which the fair implied. He touched on political affairs.

"Some people say that Dr Banda is unpopular and hated by Malawians," he said in his address, "if that was true, we in the Cabinet would have been the first to overthrow him."

Those words, or words to that effect, were amply reported to Dr Banda. Frightened out of his wits, Dr Banda started to keep a respectable distance between himself and Mr Muwalo. The first indication that Mr Muwalo was in trouble came in August when Mrs Margaret Mlanga, the head of the Women's League of the Malawi Congress Party and a close confidant of Mr Muwalo, fell from grace. She was summarily expelled from the party, stripped off all the positions she held by virtue of her status in the party, and then rushed into jail.

The symbolic significance of Mrs Mlanga's fall was clear for all to see. Another lady politician, Mrs Sadyalunda, was also expelled on trumped-up charges and locked up. Even the humble prison warders at Mikuyu tried to whisper the news to us, discreetly and in riddles. If a green tree can catch fire, what more with a dry tree, they whispered. If Mr Muwalo had failed to protect Mrs Mlanga then he himself was in trouble.

Not long after, we heard strong rumours in Mikuyu Prison that Focus Gwede himself had been placed under house arrest. Charles Ngwata, Gwede's right-hand man, escaped the net. He was merely demoted, put in uniform and posted to Thyolo District Police Station. Not long after that, we heard rumours that Dr Banda himself had taken to the national radio station to announce the immediate arrest of Mr Muwalo. According to the stories, we heard that the Malawi Police had been trailing him discreetly, the whole day, in anticipation of the radio announcement. They drove through the well-guarded fence of the Malawi Congress Party offices at Chichiri in Blantyre and sped to the office block. They rushed up the steps and surprised Mr Muwalo in his own office. Secretaries and minor clerical staff were in tears as they saw the former strong man being thrown down unceremoniously and handcuffed. That was not enough. They saw him humiliated thoroughly, as the police manhandled and tossed him into the back of a landrover, which was bristling with gun-toting members of the Police Mobile Force.

The police motorcade sped to Mr Muwalo's residence in Mount Pleasant for a thorough search. They were looking for evidence for a treason trial. After the search, Mr Muwalo was rushed to prison immediately.

Focus Gwede never went back to his office. He was arrested from his home and taken straight to prison. There were wild celebrations in all the major towns of Malawi at the news of the fall of these two people. Beer flowed copiously in the bars and night-clubs. Rightly or wrongly, people assumed that it was the end of detention-without-trial in Malawi. They mistakenly assumed that Dr Banda was a spotless angel who could do no wrong but Muwalo and Gwede were the villains who had besmirched his good image. People genuinely looked forward to a life without fear. It remained to be seen.

Mr Muwalo had two wives but that did not save him from a reputation with women. Like most powerful people, women, even married women, were attracted to him. There was very little, in fact nothing, the cuckolded husbands could do. They did not dare to quarrel with their own wives, let alone chase them out of the house for infidelity. They pretended to have seen nothing and to have heard nothing. They suffered in silence. As some people were celebrating with beer in the towns, some jubilant husbands rushed to their homes, to chase away their own wives. A number of marriages broke up that night. Husbands were no longer afraid of their own powerful wives.

The news reached us in Mikuyu but several days later. It came in dribs and drabs. The heavy flow of inmates from Zomba Prison to Mikuyu Prison ceased. It seemed as if the Special Branch had completely stopped arresting people.

On 16 November 1976, we in Cell B were startled by an unusual activity in the punishment cell which was adjacent to our yard. Welders from the Ministry of Works were busy welding extra thick bars on the tiny window. We relayed the news to the other cells through our telegraphy. Soon after this activity ended, the welders drove away. In the afternoon we heard the sound of several vehicles coming in. We immediately jumped on each other's shoulders in order to reach the tiny windows at the top. What was seen through those tiny windows was avidly described, in whispers, to those of us who were standing on the floor.

At least seven police landrovers, all of them bristling with armed policemen, stopped in front of the wire fence of the prison. From the vehicle in the middle, a man emerged. He had grown a large beard. That was the only thing seen because his head was in a cloth bag. The hood prevented him from seeing where he was going. His hands were chained. So were his legs. He walked with a great deal of difficulty because the metal chain in the legs was short. They removed the hood to enable him see where to go. Mr Muwalo's face could only be recognised by his large eyes and the partially bald head. The sideburns, which had become his hall-mark, had disappeared. He was escorted into the prison, completely surrounded by the armed men, as he walked painfully and slowly.

From the other vehicle emerged another hooded figure. The person had his hands handcuffed and his legs in chains. They removed the hood from him. He too had grown a long beard but the face of Focus Gwede was unmistakable. The rough features of his face and the patch on his head where hair failed to grow, were his hallmarks. It was unbelievable! The head of the Special Branch himself was joining the large number of political prisoners he had personally locked up. Cruel fate had turned him into one of us.

It was strange but there were no instant celebrations at Mikuyu. We were completely stunned by what was happening. We saw the power of God in all this. As far as we were concerned God was showing us that He had heard our prayers and would soon release us from bondage. He was more powerful than any powerful man. He was capable of bringing down the most mighty of men. Suddenly I remembered what Focus Gwede had said to me, in his office, nearly two years before.

"You will never get out as long as I am in this chair," he had said to me.

"Gwede, last year you were not in that chair, and you do not know if you will still be in that chair next year," I had rudely and defiantly retorted to him.

With hindsight, my words had been very prophetic. Gwede was no longer in his chair. I was entitled to expect my release the following year, on 14 May 1977, the traditional day of releases.

The Moslem friend from Mangochi, who had felt angry with me because of my analysis of the political situation, swallowed his pride and approached me.

"You were right," he said, "we are going home very soon. Long before May 14th next year. Dr Banda will use Muwalo and Gwede as scapegoats, in order to empty the prisons."

We were disappointed over one thing. Mr Muwalo was kept in

a cell of his own just as Mr Gwede was put in a cell of his own. The prison authorities correctly guessed that there was too much bitterness against these men in the other cells. They were right. I do not believe that either of these men would have been left alive, if they had been thrown in among us. They would have been beaten to death that same night.

CHAPTER 16

The Tooth

The atmosphere improved tremendously at Mikuyu, just as it had improved throughout Malawi. The gloom which had pervaded the place disappeared completely. It was an atmosphere of hope. The prison warders became more and more friendly. The incidents of brutality became few and far between.

One day, in conspiratorial whispers, one prison warder described to us in detail how he had personally humiliated Focus Gwede, the dreaded former head of the Special Branch. He had got Gwede to strip completely naked. Then he got Gwede to bend over so that he could physically inspect his anus. Meanwhile Gwede was trembling with fear, like a terrified rabbit. He did exactly as he was told. The arrogance which had characterized Gwede's personality for a long time had disappeared completely. Then he told us how they had marched him from the office, in that naked state, down to the punishment cell which was going to be his home. There, they threw him down and got his hands chained, between his chained legs. They left him like that, lying on his side, like a sack, unable to sit up or stand.

For the prison warders, the prospect of having Focus Gwede in their power was too good to be true. They too had been living in constant fear of him, as indeed were thousands of policemen and millions of Malawians.

After a few days, we too started to poke fun at the helpless Gwede, who lay chained in the punishment cell. Every movement he made got the chains clinking. We nicknamed him the bank-teller, because the chains sounded like coins being counted.

"Gwede, if you do not know God, you had better know him now," we shouted at him. "You are on a treason charge which carries a mandatory death sentence. Dr Banda is determined to hang you. Only God can save you from that death," we told him.

Others were more crude. "Gwede," they said, "now that you are here, on your way to an unmarked grave, means that I am going back to my freedom. The first thing I shall do is to hunt for all your daughters and wife. I am going to defile them, one by one."

The prison staff never trusted Gwede with anything which could be used for suicide. Even when he wanted to go to the toilet they went with him. He defecated in their full view.

One day, Gwede refused to eat his porridge. That action incensed the prison authorities. They surrounded him in the punishment cell, with their clubs at the ready. When he looked at their stern faces, he knew what they were about to do to him. He reached for the plate and ate hurriedly. His hunger strike was over before it had started.

"The bastard!" we were told gleefully a few minutes later, "how can he refuse to eat the poor food which he himself prescribed for others?" the warders told us.

During the second week of December, I received an unexpected call to the office of the Office-in-Charge. A member of the Special Branch, with a driver, had come for me.

"Give him his civilian clothes to put on!" he ordered the prison officials. They got the cloth bag out of the stores. My crumpled brown suit was pulled out. I was allowed to put on my socks and shoes.

"Let us go," he said as he led me to the car. They did not even bother to handcuff me.

As we sped towards Zomba town, the Special Branch man loosened up.

"Sam," he said to me in a very friendly manner, "I am taking you to the hospital to have your bad tooth extracted. I wish I was taking you to freedom."

"Why did it take you six months to arrange for the extraction of my tooth?"

"There are problems, Sam. The world has changed. We are struggling to keep up with the changes. Do you know that many of you at Mikuyu were going to be released last week, on 7th December?"

I could not believe what this man was saying. I was stunned.

"Release? I thought we get released only on 14th May?" I asked him incredulously.

"We have released most of the political prisoners from Zomba, Chichiri and Maula Prisons. We released them on 4th December last week. 7th December was your turn at Mikuyu. We have instructions to empty the prisons. The government has now realized that most of you are innocent."

"So, why were we not released?" I asked him, with a sigh of bitter disappointment.

"We released a large batch from Zomba Prison. One of them was a man called Bai from Likoma Island. When he reached Nkhata Bay he waited for the Ilala. Then he met a close friend of his who took him into a bar to celebrate. After a few beers, Bai started to say nasty things about Dr Banda. "He is very old and will die very soon. After torturing me for so long in his prison, I am now free," Bai boasted.

"There was a Special Branch man in the bar. He telephoned the boss about this stupidity. The boss rushed to the palace and Dr Banda got furious. He ordered that Bai should be thrown in again and that all releases should be cancelled. We sent an aeroplane to collect Bai from Nkhata Bay. He is back in prison. I tell you, it is so frustrating for us to work so hard to get thousands of you released, only to have everything derailed by a stupid drunk," sighed the Special Branch man.

I agreed with him. I felt very disappointed to realise that I might have been freed the week before. I had known Mr Bai for a long time. We were together at Chancellor College as students where he was a year behind me. It is true that he had a weak head for beer. I remember, one day, he had gone to Continental Hotel, now known as Hotel Chisakalime. It was a popular night-club with a resident band, good music and nice girls. That evening Mr Bai picked up a quarrel with a group of young men. He did not know that they were members of the Malawi Young Pioneers

Intelligence, in civilian clothes.

Be that as it may, a fisticuff fight erupted in the grounds of the hotel. Mr Bai instantly knocked down one of his assailants. He went for the throat of the second one when a long knife was plunged into his abdomen. That was the end of the fight. Mr Bai fled for dear life. A spoor of blood trailed him all along the road. His assailants chased him to finish him off but gave up after they saw how fast he ran. He fled back to Chancellor College at Chichiri but collapsed soon after Tropicana. He had lost too much blood. A sympathetic motorist picked him up and rushed him to Queen Elizabeth Central Hospital. A blood transfusion saved his life. The wound was stitched. Fortunately, no vital organ had been damaged. Mr Bai was discharged from the hospital within a week.

This incident caused another political row between the university and the establishment. The Malawi Young Pioneers, scared that it was going to be a criminal case investigated by the Police, told their Commander, Aleke Banda, a complete lie. They said that a group of university students had insulted and beaten up the Malawi Young Pioneers. They never mentioned the stabbing. Aleke Banda coloured it up a bit when he reported the incident to Dr Banda. Dr Ian Michael, the Vice Chancellor, went to report to Dr Banda about the student who was stabbed. Dr Banda received two contradictory reports of the same incident. The police corroborated the version by Dr Michel, as the proof was on a hospital bed. Aleke Banda lost a bit of his credibility but the Malawi Young Pioneers were not arrested or prosecuted.

Mr Bai received his degree two years later. He had been a lecturer at Domasi when he was thrown into prison. I did not know if it was because of drink again.

"The trouble is that we used Christmas as the appropriate Public Holiday for the releases. Now Dr Banda is completely upset. We have to convince him again. We cannot use Christmas again but the next Public Holiday is next year on 3rd March, Martyrs Day," complained the man from the Special Branch.

We drove into the fence of Zomba Prison. I was handed over to the prison authorities with instructions that I was a patient and should be put in the sick bay. I found several people in the sick bay, including Dr Peter Mwanza, the former principal of Chancellor College. He was in poor health. The atmosphere in the sick bay was a taste of freedom. There was no indication that we were in prison. The lights were not switched off at lock-up time and we slept at any time we wanted. The most exciting news that day was the appointment, into Parliament and the Cabinet by Dr Banda, of a man from Machinga who was principal of a technical college at that time. His name was Bakili Muluzi. If Dr Banda continued to load his Cabinet with educated people, we reasoned, then he was going to benefit from sound advice in the Cabinet.

In the morning, a Special Branch man came for me. He handcuffed me and led me to the car. We drove to Zomba General Hospital, across the road, where I was led to the Dental Department. The dentist was a young man. My appointment had been made already. One look at me made him very angry.

"Take those things off! I don't want my patients in handcuffs," he said authoritatively.

I could not believe what he was saying. With uncharacteristic meekness, the Special Branch man removed the handcuffs from my hands. He even apologised for the inconvenience.

"You can leave him here. You do not have to guard him in here. This place is for patients only. You can either wait for him in the car outside or come back for him after three hours," the dentist said again.

The humiliation was too much. The man from the Special Branch decided to drive away and come for me later.

I looked at the old magazines on the table in the dental surgery. I reached for one fearfully, expecting to be shouted at any time. The dentist smiled at me. That encouraged me to go ahead. That sense of freedom was so intoxicating that I felt like I had been freed from Mikuyu already. It was unbelievable! I was being treated with respect and human dignity again.

When my turn came, he put me in the chair very courteously and professionally. He put my mind at complete ease as he inspected my mouth.

"I have to give you an injection in the gums, so that you do not feel any pain when I remove the tooth," he explained to me, almost begging me for permission. I could not believe it.

He jabbed me in the gum. My jaw went numb immediately. He pulled out the pliers. When he tried to remove the bad tooth a searing pain went through me. I screamed.

"Sorry, you need another injection. You are too strong," he said apologetically.

The second injection did not help either. He had to give me three injections of the local anesthetic. Then he pulled out the bad tooth. The next tooth was also bad but the nerve was not exposed. He decided to drill that one and fill it up.

"After the anesthetic wears off, you are going to feel a lot of pain. Here are aspirin tablets to kill the pain. Here is more cotton wool to swab the blood. The bleeding will stop very soon and you need not worry about it," he said cheerfully as he finished with me.

I waited for the Special Branch man by flicking through the glossy magazines. I had not seen or touched a publication for two years. He came eventually. I spent that night in the sick bay of Zomba Prison again. The food was much better in that place but I was unable to eat because of the pain in my mouth.

The following morning I was taken back to my Cell B in Mikuyu Prison. I wasted little time before I told my fellow inmates about the failed release and Mr Bai's poor style of celebrating freedom. The news was relayed to the other cells. Our spirits were high, buoyed by hope.

CHAPTER 17

The Release

Christmas Day, 1976, came. We lined up for the customary half-mug of black tea. When lunch came we had a pleasant surprise. The relish was fresh fish cooked in oil. It was the small type of fish which is produced by fish-farmers in fish-ponds. Nothing like that had happened before. We were very excited.

On 10 January 1977, I was called to the office of the Officer-in-Charge, unexpectedly. The man from the Special Branch had come for me again.

"Give him his clothes. I am taking him away for a short time," he told the prison authorities.

I peeled off my prison uniform excitedly. For the second time in less than two months I got the thrilling feel of civilian clothes, my own clothes. We got into the car and sped for Zomba town.

"Sometimes we men forget that women are fellow human beings. They feel sexy too and would like to have a man," he said, completely out of the blue.

I did not comment as I considered the subject totally irrelevant.

"How long have you been inside, Sam?" he asked me, after a while.

"Exactly two years, after next week," I replied.

"You see, two years is too long for a woman to wait for a man," he said again.

I just did not understand what he was getting at. I did not comment. I thought his comment was irrelevant.

We reached Zomba town but did not proceed to Police Headquarters or Zomba Central Prison. The car turned into the Police Headquarters of the Eastern Division, near the University of Malawi offices. We went upstairs. They gave me a chair in a large room. They just sat me down and left me alone. What surprised me was that at least four Special Branch men, in plain clothes, occupied themselves at one end of the room.

Suddenly, the door opened. In walked a two-year-old boy, clad in a dirty, oversize T-shirt. I did not recognize my own son. The last time I had seen him was when he was still a baby in his mother's arms. The woman who walked in, behind the small boy, looked familiar but haggard and pregnant. I looked closer at her. Then the shock hit me. It was my wife. She was at least six months pregnant. There was no mistake about it. Her tummy was so large. She was followed by Miss Esnat Kadzamira, a young sister of Miss Cecilia Kadzamira, Dr Banda's official hostess. Miss Esnat Kadzamira was a Social Welfare Officer looking after destitutes in Blantyre.

"Hello darling!" my wife, Sophie, said to me as she approached me. My heart was swelling up with painful anger at her treachery. I just did not know what to say or do to her.

The four policemen stopped whatever they had been doing. They got ready to save a potentially explosive situation. That was a critical moment. They had expected me to blow up instantly and assault my wife in anger. They were there purposely to stop any murderous fight. All the hints that the Special Branch man had been making in the car were designed to prepare me for this shock.

My young son, totally oblivious of the tense situation in the room, walked over to the window, in an attempt to see the outside. The window was too high for him. He then immediately urinated on the carpet. Any attempt to stop him was futile. The urine sank into the brown carpet. The boy had struck a blow for me, against the cruel police. I was so happy, inwardly, that my son had urinated in a police officer's office. It was perverse pleasure, of course, but I felt very proud of him. I turned to my wife.

"Why did you not ask me for a divorce before you got married?" I asked her sullenly.

"I did not get married to anyone else," she replied indignantly.

"You have remarried and you are pregnant," I shouted at her.

"I am not pregnant," she lied.

I got furious.

"What games are you playing? You have been my wife. I know your body. I know you are pregnant. Why are you trying to deny the obvious? Do you think that I am a fool?" I shouted at her.

"I am not pregnant. I am still your wife," she said painfully, on the verge of tears. She looked at Miss Esnat Kadzamira, helplessly, for encouragement.

Then I realized that it was a grand conspiracy. I was the only outsider. She had been coached to lie to me about the obvious pregnancy. The entire police knew it and the entire government knew it. They had a plan about it. I suspected that even Dr Banda knew about it. They knew who had made her pregnant and wanted to protect him. It clicked in my head that the most stupid thing I could do was to act exactly the same way as they expected me to. They did not expect me to notice the pregnancy. I had better pretend that I did not notice it.

"Okay, you are not pregnant but you certainly look like you are," I said.

There was an obvious sigh of relief throughout the room. The situation was defused.

"Why did you not visit me for a whole year? I did not recognise my own son, as you saw just now," I asked her.

"I had a very bad quarrel with your aunt," she replied, and I had no option but to leave her home. I ended up as a destitute in the hands of the government. I have suffered so much in this country that I have decided to go home to Ethiopia. I shall wait for your release there," she said.

"You are contradicting yourself. How can you be a destitute and afford two tickets at the same time?" I asked her.

"The Malawi Government has given me two air tickets. One for me and the other for Joseph. But they are one way. The problem is that Joseph is a Malawian citizen and the Immigration Department will not let him go out of the country unless you, his father, give permission," she told me.

"Permission granted. Where do I sign?" I said hurriedly.

"I shall just tell them that you have agreed. That will do. In that case may I say good-bye darling. We are booked to fly out to

Addis Ababa the day after tomorrow, on the 12th January."

I could not bear to shake her hand, let alone kiss her. I got hold of Joseph my son and hugged him. Then I shook his hand.

"Good-bye!" I said to him. "We shall be together soon."

My wife felt relieved to escape hurriedly from a very awkward situation. She had expected me to be justifiably angry with her.

I left for Mikuyu Prison, soon after they left for Blantyre. I was a very bitter and angry man. I felt badly let down by the very person I had given my heart to. I realized that my deeply cherished marriage was irreparably destroyed. There was no way I was going to look at my wife with the same pride, respect, honour and love I had for her before. Most likely I was going to think of her as a cheap, despicable, loose woman who was not much above a prostitute. My heart was broken.

Was I going to be able to forgive her? My thoughts wandered over to my son. No matter what, I was not going to lose that son. I was not going to let him be brought up by some slob of a step-father.

Deep down in my heart, I suspected that I was on the list of the first group to be released from Mikuyu Prison. I suspected that the Police did not want me to come home and be confronted with a nasty, marital problem. They thought that it would be better to get my wife out of the country, in order to give me time for reflection. My suspicions were confirmed by the fact that they had not thought of sending her away earlier and the fact that they were suddenly showing so much concern for the family of a detainee.

I learned, later on, that my wife had been raped. At the Social Welfare Offices in Blantyre, near Kwacha Conference Centre, where my wife and son were, was a perverted Social Welfare Officer who came from a family with a history of sexual perversion. One of his brothers was in jail for murder, after he brutally beat his own wife to death over a disagreement about sex. The brother who raped my wife went to the helpless woman he was supposed to look after and blackmailed her. He was not going to give her the Red Cross-donated powdered milk which my young son needed badly. Due to the poor diet and harsh living conditions, my wife's body was not able to give the child sufficient breast milk. "Milk for sex or nothing at all," he said. When the blackmail failed he went to rape her in the hostel at night. She became pregnant.

She got the courage to write a letter to Wadson Deleza, who was the Minister for Labour and Social Welfare at that time. Mr Deleza got too scared to discipline the man because he was a fellow Sena with Gwanda Chakuamba, a powerful regional minister for the south. Between them they decided to protect the man by getting rid of my wife. Meanwhile, the man himself had been desperately pleading with my wife to take some roots for an abortion. My wife suspected murder and refused. She was then told, out of the blue, that the Government of Malawi would give her and her son air tickets back to Ethiopia where she could abort the pregnancy in a hospital. That way, me, the husband, would never know about it and her marriage would be saved while the rapist would keep his Civil Service job. That was the conspiracy which led me to the strange farewell between me and my young family at the Police Headquarters of the Eastern Division. They had realized that what the rapist had done was more than enough provocation for mass murder, especially for a man who was suffering unjustifiably in prison. They did not expect me to notice the pregnancy. As a result, I would have never known about the expected abortion. My own wife was persuaded to be a party to the deceit, in order to save her marriage, but in reality it was to save the rapist's job. Anywhere else such a rapist would have gone to jail for many years. In Malawi, raping a detainee's wife was not a crime, apparently.

Back in Mikuyu, the days passed by, slowly and painfully. January came to an end. We started February 1977.

Both Mr Muwalo and Mr Gwede had their case opened at the Traditional Court in Blantyre. They were jointly charged with high treason and accused of attempting to take over the government unconstitutionally. The evidence was flimsy and would never have sufficed in a normal court of law, but that was precisely why they were sent to the Traditional Court. The traditional chiefs did not know any law. They knew in advance of the trial what sentence to pass. Broad hints were given to them.

It was a hurried court case. They had no chance whatsoever. They were not allowed any legal representation. Even if they had been allowed some legal representation, they would have been unable to pay for such services. Both men had already been placed under the provisions of the Forfeiture Act. Their personal and business assets, including clothing, forks and cameras were seized and auctioned off to realize cash for the State. Their bank accounts were also frozen and the money taken by the State.

Both Mrs Muwalo and Mrs Gwede were also locked up, without trial. Their children, almost overnight, had become without parents, penniless and homeless. That was the full wrath of Dr Banda, against the very people he had callously used for many years.

The first time they were taken from Mikuyu, to the court in Blantyre, was on 25 January 1977, the anniversary of my interrogation by Focus Gwede in his office two years before. A long line of vehicles, full of armed policemen, used to fetch them in the morning and bring them back in the evening.

A death sentence was passed on both men at the end of the trial. It was mandatory on conviction. Both men appealed against conviction and sentence, which served only to postpone the day of execution. In August 1977, less than a year after arrest, Mr Muwalo was hanged hurriedly together with other criminals in Zomba Prison. Focus Gwede escaped death by a whisker. His death sentence was commuted to life at Dr Banda's discretion.

On 26 February 1977, we were sitting around in the yard of our Cell B when a large, black rat ran down the storm-water drain which passed by our cell. It was unusual. We had never seen rats at Mikuyu before. The rat was in a state of agitation and had come from the direction of the prison storeroom. Our civilian clothes were stored there.

Some of us were very excited to see that huge rat. We thought that it was a very auspicious sign. That rat had been eating our clothes in the storeroom over the years, totally undisturbed. The fact that the rat had fled from its home meant that someone else was there to disturb the bags. What other disturbance was there, than that our bags were being sorted out, to give us our clothes on release day?

It was far-fetched but we believed it. Some of our fellow inmates did not want to believe this very sound analysis of the harmless incident of an agitated rat. We passed on the news to the other cells anyway.

On 28 February, two days later, we were allowed to go for showers in the afternoon. At four o'clock we were locked up, as usual. We were about to settle down to our indoor games when the entire prison staff came back and opened the cell door. Outside in the courtyard were dozens of the white cloth-bags which contained our personal clothes. It was the release day!

"Anyone who hears his name must immediately take his blanket and walk out!" said the Officer-in-Charge.

We all paid serious attention, as he started reading out the names. I heard my name. I rose up, overcome by joy, and dashed for the door. There was no time or need for saying farewells. Only eighteen were left behind in Cell B. Out in the courtyard, we eagerly peeled off the prison uniform, to put on our personal clothes. Then the inmates from the other cells poured out to join us. A total of two-hundred-and-seventy-four inmates were released that night. It was the largest group ever. It was a time of goodwill and for tears of joy. We sought each other out for congratulations and farewells.

Even the prison warders were immensely relieved. Some of them could not resist the temptation to show their joy at our release. I removed a tie from my shirt and gave it to one warder who had asked me for a memento.

It was past midnight when they finished processing us. After giving us our clothes they gave us the money they had kept for us. This was the money we had on us on the day of arrest. Then they gave us our valuables such as wrist-watches and wedding-rings.

Members of the Special Branch were there in full force, partly to see us off and partly to ensure that those who were left behind did not riot. They had brought several open trucks to take us to Zomba town. Even at that stage we had some tearful tragedies. Some of the released political prisoners, particularly those who had five years or more, were virtually naked. Their personal clothes had decayed in the cloth bags and just fell to pieces in the owners' hands. The prison officials looked for some discarded uniforms of their own to give the embarrassed men.

Due to the late hour of the finalization of the release process, it was decided that we be taken to the second Mikuyu Prison where convicted prisoners were kept. It was about half a kilometre away. A special cell was evacuated and given to us. None of us could believe it when the door was left open. But then, none of us slept either. We sang religious songs and said prayers of thanks all night long.

In the morning, on 1 March, we were driven to the Police Headquarters in Zomba. Mac Kamwana, the Inspector General of Police, was in high spirits and could not let the opportunity to address us pass. Instead of giving us bus warrants we were given open trucks. A truck for the south towards Blantyre and beyond. A truck towards the north, up to Mangochi. A truck for the north towards Lilongwe and beyond.

I jumped on the truck to Blantyre. We were a curious sight to many people. At Njuli a rain storm hit us. We were all drenched. It was quite sunny in Limbe when I dropped off at the Post Office. The thought of being seen by friends and relatives, in that terrible condition, was disturbing. I had K10 on me on the day of my arrest. I used it to get a taxi. I felt secure in a taxi rather than being an object of curious glances. As soon as I was out of town, I stopped the taxi, paid off the driver and walked the rest of the way to my aunt's home in Chief Somba's area.

"Cousin has come!" my young cousin shouted excitedly when I reached my aunt's home.

"Shut up, you fool! Don't you know that he is going through a terrible hell on this earth?" I heard his mother, my aunt, shout at him angrily.

She did not believe what the boy was saying until she laid her own eyes on me. Then she nearly collapsed with shock. It was true. I was back home. Both my wife and my son were not there, but I was free at last.